SERENGETI SERENDIPITY

❧

FROM THE DEPTHS OF DESPAIR TO THE HEIGHTS OF KILIMANJARO

MICHAEL DELPORT

Ark House Press
arkhousepress.com

© 2025 Michael Delport

Some names and identifying details have been changed to protect the privacy of individuals.

Cataloguing in Publication Data:
Title: Serengeti Serendipity
ISBN: 978-1-7642813-7-9 (pbk)
Subjects: BIO026000   BIOGRAPHY & AUTOBIOGRAPHY / Memoirs; REL012170
RELIGION / Christian Living / Personal Memoirs; REL012040   RELIGION / Christian
Living / Inspirational.

Design by initiateagency.com

For my family – immediate and extended,
near and far, present and future and yet to be born.
May you carry the spirit of adventure in your veins
the courage to take the first step,
and the joy of walking life's journeys together.
Keep chasing mountains,
keep chasing meaning and never forget:
the greatest adventure is the walk of faith.

Contents

SERENGETI NATIONAL PARK —
DECEMBER 2023: THE STORY BEGINS

SECTION ONE — THE SPARK:
WHEN THE MOUNTAIN CALLED

SECTION TWO — THE SETBACK:
WHEN THE BODY SAID NO

SECTION THREE — THE CLIMB: WE SUMMIT TOGETHER

CONCLUSION / EPILOGUE

VOICES FROM THE JOURNEY

Introduction

This story was never mine alone. Along the way, others shaped it – through care, encouragement, or simply being there at the right time. That's why this book begins with four short forewords: a doctor I met by chance, a Tanzanian host who believed, a sister who witnessed it all and a friend and business partner who saw the transformation up close.

Together, their voices frame what follows: a story not only of mountains and setbacks, but of resilience, community and connection.

Foreword – *Dr. Mario Hanke*
The Doctor by Chance

Is forty minutes enough to really see into a person? I believe it is.

The morning after I had stood on the summit of Kilimanjaro, still weary but full of joy, I walked into the dining room at Springlands Hotel. Michael invited me to join him for lunch. As we sat together, he began to share his story: the dream of climbing Africa's highest mountain and the sudden medical emergency in the Serengeti that brought that dream to a halt.

By chance – or perhaps by something greater – he was sharing this with a urologist. He had just endured a frightening ordeal and now faced the uncertainty of what lay ahead. In that short time, I was able to explain what had happened to his body, outline the kind of surgery he would likely need and give him confidence that a full recovery – and a second chance at the mountain – was possible.

What impressed me most was not the setback, but his resolve to return. Many would have accepted defeat; Michael chose another way.

This book is the result of that choice. It shows that even when dreams collapse, they can be rebuilt. It is about resilience, courage and the power of believing that after you get well, anything is possible again.

– Dr. Mario Hanke
Urologist, Germany

Foreword – *Zainab "Mama Zara" Ansell*
The Host Who Believed

Over the years, Zara Tours has welcomed many climbers from around the world. Some reach the summit of Kilimanjaro, some do not. But every journey has meaning, and every story is important.

Michael's story is one I will never forget. On his first visit, his dream of standing on *The Roof of Africa* was interrupted in the Serengeti, in the most unexpected way. Alongside the care we gave, there were also remarkable moments of timing. It was a frightening setback, but even then, I could see his determination. Before he left, he promised he would return.

One year later, he did – and not alone. He came back with a group of friends inspired by his story. Together they climbed, laughed, struggled and stood at Uhuru Peak. For me, this was not only a victory for

Michael, but a reminder of what Kilimanjaro teaches us: the mountain is not just about altitude, it is about attitude.

This book captures that truth. It is about resilience; second chances and the bonds formed between those who choose to climb together. As Tanzanians, we are honoured to be part of such journeys.

May Michael's story remind you, that no matter the setbacks, there is always another summit waiting.

– Zainab "Mama Zara" Ansell
Founder & CEO, Zara Tours

Foreword – *Michelle Delport*
The Sister Who Witnessed It All

When we gathered in Mossel Bay, South Africa to scatter our dad's ashes, Kilimanjaro transformed from a distant dream into something real – a way to honour life and step boldly into the unknown. I imagined standing beside Michael on that summit, sharing a moment that would connect us to something greater than ourselves.

But life had other plans.

In the Serengeti, just days before our planned climb, I watched my brother face a crisis that filled me with a dread I'd never experienced. When I heard him say, "I would check myself into a hospital if I was home," my heart broke. This wasn't just about losing the mountain – it was about potentially losing him.

I did what I could to support him through those terrifying hours, but it was Michael's fierce determination that truly carried him through. His strength in the face of a gruelling operation and long recovery awed me then and it still does now. While we never did stand together on

Kilimanjaro's summit, watching him return a year later and achieve that dream filled me with immense pride.

Eighteen months later, climbing Mount Fuji together – his health restored, his spirit soaring – I felt a joy that words can barely capture. As we shared those slopes as a family, I knew with certainty that the adventure spirit burns bright in the Delports, stronger than any setback.

This book is about climbing mountains, but it's also about the resilience it takes to conquer life's unexpected challenges. Michael's journey, from a hospital bed to a mountaintop, proves that setbacks don't erase dreams – they reshape them into something even more meaningful.

I hope his courage inspires you as it continues to inspire me.

– Michelle Delport
Sister

Foreword – *Greg Anderson*
The Friend Who Saw the Journey

Michael's deeply personal and vulnerable account of his life-or-death experience in the heart of southern Africa reads like a Wilbur Smith novel – rich with perilous choices, agonizing uncertainties and moments of unexpected serendipity.

These pivotal "sliding door" moments form the core of this remarkable journey – an exploration not only of the treacherous situation he faced, but of the mountains, both literal and metaphorical, that he wanted to climb. In doing so, Michael offers us a compelling portrait of a life fully examined.

His story is one of turning stumbling blocks into steppingstones. The practical insights woven through these pages make this more than just an adventure; it's a thought-provoking and inspiring read that captures the very essence of Michaels journey in life so far.

– Greg Anderson
Friend & Business Partner of 25 Years

WHY I HAD TO WRITE THIS

This is not the book I thought I would write.

When the idea of climbing Mount Kilimanjaro first surfaced, I pictured a simple adventure story with a neat arc: training, travelling, climbing, summiting, celebrating. A mountain conquered, a dream fulfilled. Something crossed off my bucket list.

But life had other plans.

What unfolded instead was a story of interruption, resilience and return. It began with a medical emergency in the Serengeti – an ordeal that left me grounded, catheterised and facing surgery rather than the summit I had come for. That unexpected detour forced me to ask new questions: about health, about courage, about timing and about what really matters.

I decided to write this book because too many things happened that I couldn't simply dismiss as coincidences. The way help arrived at exactly the right moments, the doors that opened when they should have been closed – it was all too precise, too timely. Some stories need to be remembered, passed on for family, friends and others to read. Mine is one of those stories – the kind that makes you pause and ask whether life is really just a string of coincidences, or whether there might be something more.

What I know is that I had to tell it.

This is my first book, and I have to say I've enjoyed the journey. I write as a husband, father, brother and friend who had his plans turned upside down in Africa and who discovered that the interruption gave the story its meaning.

My hope is that as you read, you'll see echoes of your own story. Maybe you've had dreams interrupted, plans overturned, or health scares that reminded you how fragile life can be. Maybe you've wondered if you'd ever get another chance at something you thought was lost. If so, I hope this book encourages you.

I hope it stirs the adventurous spirit in you, prompts honest reflection about health and above all, helps you wrestle with the deeper question of what gives life its real meaning.

With heartfelt thanks to everyone who shared this journey with me. This book is as much yours as it is mine.

Welcome to *Serengeti Serendipity*.

Michael Delport
Brisbane, Australia, 2025

michael@serengetiserendepity.com
www.serengetiserendipity.com

ABOUT THE AUTHOR

M ichael Delport, South African-born, first landed in Australia in 1981 for a Rotary Exchange year. After returning home for further studies and 15 months of compulsory national service, he immigrated to Australia at the end of 1984. Today he barracks for Australia when they take on South Africa - proof that anything can change. He's a big believer that life should be full of firsts. Whether you're in your 30s, 60s, or anywhere in between, it's never too late to take on something new.

He has spent more than 35 years in financial planning, 25 in property development and the last 15 focused on consultancy. Through his company, the Delport Group, he helps people take their next steps in business, property and life. His career began with AMP in 1990, moving from insurance agent to Certified Financial Planner, before expanding into property development in 2000. Along the way he completed his Diploma of Financial Planning from RMIT and an Executive MBA from the University of Sydney.

Michael now lives in Queensland with Vicki, his wife of more than 40 years. They have two married children and love any time spent together as a family. Outside of work, he enjoys a physical challenge, squash, swimming, hiking and the occasional nail-biting sporting finish.

After a **setback in the Serengeti** scuttled his first attempt to climb Kilimanjaro, Michael regrouped and returned. A year later, with a great group of friends and a lot more perspective, he stood at the summit. His personal faith was deeply tested during his Serengeti experience...

Serengeti Serendipity is his debut book - a memoir born from that detour in Tanzania and a triumphant return to the summit of Kilimanjaro. It is a story of resilience, community, second chances, and a life forever changed.

WHAT TO EXPECT

The book opens with my story from the Serengeti – a moment when adventure turned into survival and everything changed. Looking back, I can see that along the way, there were countless moments of **serendipity**, coincidence, or something more. Except for one unmistakable occasion, I don't stop to point them out. Instead, I leave it to you, the reader, to decide how many there are – and what they mean.

From there, the story circles back to where it all began – the spark of an idea, the first commitments and the setbacks that came before the climb. The journey then continues to unfold in sequence, carrying you step by step toward the summit of Kilimanjaro. Along the way, the Serengeti thread returns to be completed, tying the opening story back into the whole.

What follows is more than just a mountain story about climbing *The Roof of Africa*. It's a story about interruptions and returns, about health and resilience, about family, friendship and the ripple effect of a dream shared.

Woven through all of it is the adventurous spirit – not reserved for mountaineers or explorers, but alive in anyone who dares to step beyond comfort, face a setback and keep moving forward.

And so, the journey begins, on a night in the Serengeti when everything changed.

Welcome to *Serengeti Serendipity*.

Michael Delport

SERENGETI
NATIONAL PARK
DECEMBER 2023

The Story Begins

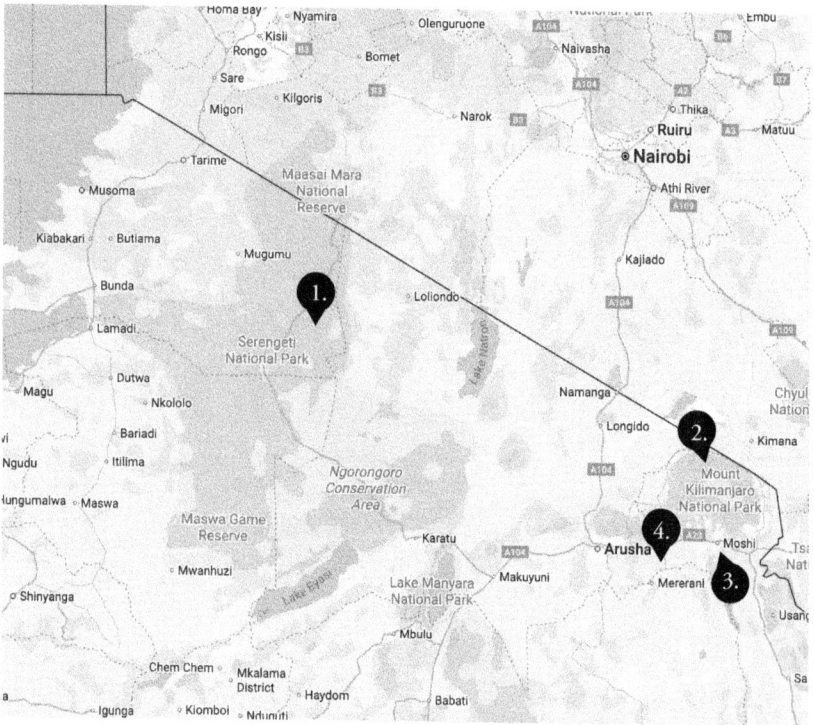

Tanzania

Map courtesy of Google Maps

---

1. Seronera Airport

3. Moshi

2. Mount Kilimanjaro (elv. 5895m)

4. Kilimanjaro International Airport

CHAPTER ONE

SHATTERED DREAMS &
WEAKENED STREAMS

The Serengeti was asleep, I wasn't.

Just after midnight, I was standing barefoot in front of the toilet, a tidy safari bungalow setup with a cool concrete floor and the odd spider for company. I looked out the small window – the camp stillness unforgettable, the moon doing its thing overhead.

I was in real pain. Struggling to urinate. A strong, burning sensation. And whatever came out was more of a trickle than a stream. It had me up three or four times that night – restless, uncomfortable and quietly starting to be concerned.

I was on a five-day safari with my sister Michelle. We'd already enjoyed two days of incredible game viewing – and now, we were just three days away from starting an epic Mount Kilimanjaro adventure.

Did I mention this was only three days before we were meant to tackle... *The Roof of Africa – Uhuru Peak, 5895 meters.* After at least three decades of dreaming, I was committed. Hard to explain, but I knew I was ready. I could feel it.

That said, I was nervous too. Thousands take on the challenge each year, with a 70 to 80 percent success rate, depending on the route chosen, fitness etc. Still, I was excited.

What made it even more exciting was that I wasn't doing it alone. Thanks to the adventurous spirit in our extended family, earlier that year my sister, Michelle, and brother-in-law, Anton (my sister Emmy's husband), had committed to the climb too. We would take on the highest free-standing mountain in the world, together.

The next morning at breakfast, I shared my struggle with Michelle. I told her I'd been up every ninety minutes since midnight – not much coming out, just the tiniest amount each time and a burning sensation while trying. If I had to guess, maybe the thickness of one finger at the bottom of a glass – no more than about 30 millilitres.

We've always found it easy to talk about just about anything, so there was no awkwardness – just silent concern and a hope that this was a minor hiccup that wouldn't affect our adventure.

I self-diagnosed it as possibly a urinary tract infection, given the burning sensation and the fact that I was still recovering from food poisoning picked up on my way to Tanzania. Three days earlier, after arriving at the Springlands Hotel in Moshi I'd seen a doctor, to get treatment for the food poisoning. He had given me antibiotics and suggested I stop taking the anti-malaria tablets, which I did. He also encouraged me to keep my fluid intake up, to remain hydrated and help my body heal.

Regardless of my nighttime difficulties, Michelle and I decided to go ahead with our planned safari. We had a quick word with Zamoyoni, who had introduced himself as Zamo, our driver-guide, to let him know

I'd need more stops than usual. He had our ride ready: one of Zara Tours' old workhorses – forest green, Toyota Land Cruiser Troop Carrier.

Dust-caked and battle-tested from years on the Serengeti, it wasn't built for comfort – two low individual seats up front, a higher bench behind – that required whoever sat there to crouch if they wanted to see through the windscreen. Most of the time, it was easier to pop up the canvas roof, stand and enjoy 360-degree game viewing. But with just the three of us, it felt like we had the whole park to ourselves.

Michelle and I took turns riding up front in the best seat. I was still trying to go whenever I could across the day, with very little success. At least the painkillers were doing their job and I was being distracted by game.

I reckon I tried four or five times that day – maybe more, but I wasn't keeping count.

We were barely an hour into the drive when nature delivered one of those unforgettable scenes. We'd pulled up to watch a pride of lions lounging on a cluster of boulders, several stories higher than our vehicle and only about a hundred metres from the 4WD. They looked completely at ease – like kings surveying their territory. It was Africa: wild, real and totally unhurried.

But… I needed to go again.

Zamo, rightfully cautious, wasn't keen on me going behind the vehicle as usual. He reminded us that the animals see the whole vehicle as one body – rather than the individuals inside it. Stepping away from the shape of the cruiser would make me stand out and possibly make me look like lunch. Instead, he had me step out and stand in front of the left-side door, facing away from the lions, with my back to him and Michelle, who both stayed in the car.

There I was, out in the open, painfully trying to relieve myself, while a pride of lions looked on from their rocky perch. If it wasn't so uncomfortable, it would've made for a cracking story – which, I suppose, it now is.

After approximately six hours – and about four urinary stops out in the wilderness – seeing everything from majestic birdlife to a rare moment involving a herd of impalas, we made our way back to the lodge. I was looking forward to making use of the bath in our upgraded accommodation – courtesy of Mama Zara herself, the warm and quietly formidable woman who owned the tour company organising both our safari and mountain climb.

I had met her the day before the start of our safari.

By now, it had been about 18 hours since the first signs of trouble the night before. I was needing to go almost hourly, still with very little output. I kept drinking water – like we're all told to do – flushing out the food poisoning, staying hydrated, keeping strong for the climb. A good thing – at least, that's what I told myself.

The bath helped me relax, but it did nothing for the symptoms.

With our Kilimanjaro climb was fast approaching, I was choosing to stay positive. It was just over two days away and I didn't want anything derailing it: not for me and definitely not for Michelle. I kept thinking it would sort itself out. However, it didn't. Not even a little.

That evening at dinner, I said something to Michelle that changed everything, "Michelle, something's not right. If I was back home, I know I'd be checking myself into a hospital."

I was ten thousand miles from home – Brisbane, Australia. In the middle of the Serengeti. More than a day's drive from any clinic. It wasn't just the pain now – it was the sense that something was seriously off. We decided to ask Zamo to join us at our table and let him in on the full story. He'd already seen me struggling during the day, so it didn't take much to bring him up to speed.

Before we could even ask about changing plans, he said, "There's a doctor onsite at this Safari Lodge. I'll go and ask him to join us."

Wait – what?

I just sat there, stunned. A doctor? Here? At this lodge? In the middle of nowhere? We weren't even meant to be at the lodge. We'd only been upgraded from a glamping site few days earlier after I my chance meeting with Mama Zara.

While Zamo went off to find the doctor, I took the chance to make yet another painful trip to the men's – burning sensation and all.

No more than fifteen minutes later, Dr Godwin joined us at the dinner table. It was surreal. We filled him in on everything from the past five days. When he heard that the doctor I'd seen back in Moshi was Dr Haggai, he smiled – they were good friends.

After reviewing the medications, asking questions about the antibiotics, the malaria tablets (which I had stopped), my painkillers and water intake, he said, "Let's test for a UTI. Right now."

He handed me a jar – a little smaller than a coke can, with no volume markings on it. Off I went again – this time, oddly relieved to be doing so for a purpose. I managed a small sample – not more than a thickness of small finger at the bottom, no more. Which he took straight back to his office to run test. Amazing that he had the equipment in the middle of the Serengeti to take the tests.

No forms. No waiting. No lab courier. No wait for a return call in 72 hours.

About half an hour later, Dr Godwin returned to the table with the results, "Michael, you don't have a urinary tract infection. But can I ask – do you have a history of prostate issues?"

Retrospectively, I'm surprised I hadn't already considered it. I had been diagnosed with a benign enlarged prostate (BEP) five years earlier. At the time, I thought it was around 100cc – roughly three times the average size. In my defence, I had been thorough with all my medical preparation leading into this trip. As part of my training and health checks just to be thorough, I'd even seen my urologist six months earlier to double check that my benign enlarged prostate wouldn't interfere with climbing Kilimanjaro. He'd cleared me and even offered medication to help reduce the nighttime urge to go...

Dr Godwin nodded as I shared this.

He then explained that he suspected the first two days of bumpy 4WD, driving through the game parks, had caused the prostate to press harder against the urethra – creating a partial blockage. It made complete sense. Finally, we had an explanation.

He told us we'd need to abandon the safari and head back to Moshi first thing in the morning. He planned to call Dr Haggai and get things organised. I would now need to *reduce* my fluid intake, and we'd aim to get help as soon as we arrived. He did mention that there is medication to help relax the prostate, but we all knew I did not have the luxury of time on my side to benefit from such medication. I needed urgent relief.

It was a comfort to now have a plan. As difficult as it was, I was still managing to pass the smallest amount – no more than trickle each time. We finally knew what we were dealing with – and that I needed to get to a clinic ASAP to get some relief; though what 'relief' might look like, I still wasn't sure.

It was around 10pm by the time we had a plan – about 22 hours since the first signs of trouble. Zamo agreed we'd travel back the next day, leaving just after sunrise. It would be a quick breakfast, check-out and then an all-day drive back to Moshi. He estimated 8 to 10-hour hours, depending on road conditions and other vehicles. It wouldn't be comfortable – but it would get me closer to help.

That night was one of the longest I can remember. I barely slept. The urges came every 20 to 30 minutes. I lost count of how many times I tried to go during those eight hours. I couldn't tell you how much of my Kilimanjaro supply of painkillers I chewed through. I just know I was in a blur of misery – exhausted, hurting, restless. At some point during the night, I packed my suitcase, I needed something to do. I wanted to be ready the moment the first sign of light hit the horizon.

Morning couldn't come soon enough. Bags loaded, I skipped coffee and drank as little as possible – the complete opposite of everything we'd been taught for mountain training. The staff were kind. They knew something was wrong and helped with an early breakfast and smooth checkout.

It was now 30 hours since my first failure to urinate properly. Climbing into the vehicle, I slid into the front seat. Michelle insisted I take it. We'd been taking turns the previous three days during the safari, but she wasn't having it this time. Zamo told us that the doctors would coordinate with one another and with us, during the day.

We were heading back the way we had come, just much faster – along the *onvergeetlike Serengeti grond paaie* (Afrikaans for 'unforgettable Serengeti dirt roads'). Funny how easy the Afrikaans comes back to me when I'm back on African soil – especially in moments like this. Though honestly, those roads felt less unforgettable and more unforgiving now. The last place I wanted to be.

Zamo picked up the pace compared to our first three days – understandably, we were no longer consciously scanning the bush for lions or leopards. To his credit, he still drove with care. He didn't like speeding through the park – not because of the roads, but because he didn't want to hit any wildlife. Michelle and I both assured him he should stick to what-ever speed he felt comfortable with, even if it was slower than the limit.

Only 20 minutes into the drive, I had the urge again. I did the maths. If I needed to stop every 20 minutes for a five-minute pit stop, we'd be adding hours to what was already expected to be an 8 to 10-hour journey. I was in trouble.

Michelle saw it on my face. Leaning forward between the front seats, she sincerely encouraged me. I don't remember exactly what she said, but I remember appreciating her support, encouragement, sisterly care, "Michael… you can do this. Just please don't explode."

I slumped down, head bowed, trying to find a position that lessened the pain. And I remember a silent prayer – not a polished, reflective kind of prayer – a desperate one. "God, please… I need a miracle; I need to fly out of here!"

Forty minutes into the journey, the pain became unbearable. I asked Zamo to pull over. He asked me to hold on just a little longer – just five minutes.

"There's a building coming up on the left – it has toilets. Better than stopping here, the road is busy with safari vehicles" he said. Only five minutes. Can I do it? I said, "Okay, I will try."

We pulled in. As we approached, he casually mentioned, "This is the Serengeti airport, Seronera."

What?

Standing at the urinal inside the tiny terminal, one thought pre-vailed through my pain and frustration: *is there a flight out of here?*

I walked straight to the counter. Calmly – or at least pretending to be – I asked if there was a flight to an airport near Moshi, where Dr Haggai would be waiting for me.

SHATTERED DREAMS & WEAKENED STREAMS

"There is a flight to Arusha in about 45 minutes – maybe an hour," the man said. "A few seats left – it will be two hundred and fifty US dollars."

Done deal.

He asked me to take a seat and said he'd call me once the ticket was sorted. Still at the counter, I asked how long the flight would be. I was very aware that small planes don't have toilets. He told me it would be about 40-minute flight.

No more dirt roads to bounce along, but a new challenge was becoming rather apparent. At that point, my intervals were down to 20 to 25 minutes, and I knew I'd just barely managed the 45-minute road trip to get here. Somehow, I would hold on again – and now I was doing the maths again. If I timed it right, I might just make it… as long as the plane didn't taxi like it had all day to take off, or circle Arusha waiting for a slot to land.

Still, it was a much better plan than ten-plus hours on the dirt roads.

Before taking a seat where he asked me to wait, I walked back to the vehicle to share the incredible news with Michelle and Zamo. Naturally, they had been wondering what was taking so long – especially when I was only capable of a trickle. I gave them the update and collected my luggage.

It was still hard to believe – not only had we stumbled upon an airport in the middle of the Serengeti, but I was also about to board a plane to get medical help. I was glad I'd waited the extra five minutes and managed one more attempt at the toilet – every drop counted.

Looking back, and even in that moment, I deeply appreciated Michelle's shift in focus during those crucial hours. She had quietly put our safari on pause and made sure my needs came first. It was not about the safari trip anymore; it was about getting me sorted. That was love in action – it was caring. Thank you.

We took a few minutes to say goodbye. No drama. Just a shared understanding that this was the right call. I'd get help faster and she could now continue the safari as planned – in the front seat, back to enjoying the wildlife... A strange kind of win-win. We'd regroup in Moshi before our scheduled Kilimanjaro briefing with Festo, the leader of the team of porters, the next evening. That was still the plan, after all.

Back inside the airport, I sat in the waiting area, ten metres from the men's toilet – watching my fluid intake, the clock and my dwindling supply of pain killers. Everything else ceased to matter. No matter how much I try and remember the details of my surroundings now, I just can't.

It's amazing how small one's world becomes when there's a serious medical challenge. I know we had an exciting animal sighting after leaving the lodge that morning – something ordinarily worth remembering – but, for the life of me, I couldn't tell you what it was.

I was no longer the observant secret agent, taking in every detail of the landscape. I'd been reduced to a man on a mission – with one very specific and increasingly urgent objective... get on the plane, hold on without resorting to wetting my pants.

While waiting, I finally had a moment to think about everything that had happened over the last 32 hours. One thing puzzled me: why hadn't the idea of flying out come up at dinner the night before? We'd even heard an incredible story from Dr Godwin – how, just a few months earlier, a man from Denmark had to be helicoptered out because he couldn't urinate at all. That detail stuck with me.

So why didn't flying out cross anyone's mind? I suspect the cost of the helicopter played a part and maybe the fact that I was still getting some relief – even if it was a painful trickle.

Looking back, I realise now I was not thinking in straight lines. I wasn't picking up on animals, landscapes, or even options. My world had shrunk to pain, urgency, and endurance. What might seem obvious in hindsight just didn't surface in the moment. And maybe that's what happens when you're in it. The 'obvious' no longer is seen.

About 20 minutes before departure, the man from the counter came back and asked for my luggage. In return, he handed me what looked like a large wooden paddle – maybe 12 centimetres long, with some faded paint on the end.

"Give this to the guy at the plane," he said. No boarding pass. No receipt. Just the paddle.

Classic. It triggered memories of growing up in Africa – how easy it is to get things done when there's less fuss over formalities.

I watched the baggage handler walk my suitcase over to the small plane – maybe a twelve-seater –parked out front. Five minutes later, the same man asked me to follow him. On the way to the counter, he turned and asked for the cash – $250. There was a brief awkward moment. It wasn't exactly a counter transaction.

There was no mistaking what this looked like. 'Allegedly', of course.

Good thing I'd brought US dollars to tip the porters after the Kilimanjaro climb. I handed over the cash, clutched my paddle and hoped for the best. My bag was already lined up alongside the others.

Walking toward the plane, I pointed out my luggage to the handler. Boarding was easy – no boarding pass needed, just climbed in after giving back the wooden paddle.

You've got to love Africa... I do!

A few passengers were scattered through the rows in front. So, I grabbed a seat in the back row on the right, and with one vacant seat beside me.

The plane was a small twin-prop with fourteen seats in total, including the two pilot seats up front. Four rows were for passengers; with single seats on the left of each row and two on the right. No overhead storage, no toilet and no food service – just a narrow central strip to walk down, ducking your head and watching your elbows and knees.

You could see straight through to the cockpit – no door, no curtain, just two pilots with the usual headsets on. The windows were rounded and small – great for spotting game.

As we taxied out, about two hours after first arriving at the airport and almost 35 hours into my ordeal, the pilot greeted his passengers. He made an announcement:

"There's been a change with the flight plan. We'll first drop off a passenger at the southern Serengeti, then head north to pick someone up before flying on to Arusha."

Ag nie (oh, no)! A bigger challenge.

What started as a challenge of managing one flight had now tripled in complexity. What was supposed to be a 40-minute flight had now become nearly two hours in the air: 25 minutes south, 40 minutes north and 35 minutes to Arusha – plus two stops. Over two hours instead of a 40-minute flight.

There was no way for me – to let anyone know about the change – no signal, no phone call. I just had to trust that Zamo, with his satellite phone, would alert the right people... And, that they would find out about the flight change because there was no way to reach them.

As we descended toward the southern airstrip, flying low over a famous river crossing – the one from the David Attenborough documentaries, where zebras and wildebeest migrate and crocodiles wait for the next feed. It had only been 20 minutes, and I badly needed to go. Again.

Desperately.

As we lined up for the approach, I leaned forward sitting on the edge of my seat and asked the question like I was ordering a coffee, though my voice was a bit tighter than usual,

"Excuse me… would it be okay if I used the toilet when we land?"

"Yes, not a problem," the pilot replied calmly.

It was the answer I hoped for. I'd already committed to holding on. Another three to five more minutes. That's all I needed. No need to wet my pants just yet.

I looked ahead and spotted a small building near the runway that look like a toilet block, holding back the joy of realising it was not long before I would get the relief. My body was busting, and I needed stronger pain killers. We dropped lower. I braced.

And then – suddenly – the engines roared, and the plane started climbing again.

We were circling.

Nooooo… What's going on?

The first approach had been aborted – the pilot was chasing wildlife off the runway, hundreds of different kinds of buck, mainly wildebeest and zebras scattering in every direction. Second attempt pending.

My three-minute wait turned into a ten-minute test. And I was right back in the same desperate space I'd been in earlier that morning, in the vehicle, doing everything I could to hold on...

Crazy experience.

Finally, we landed. I had to wait my turn being very careful not to push anybody while disembarking. I jogged toward the building I'd spotted earlier – about 100 meters away – the same one someone had pointed out to me when disembarking. I made it to the first door and found myself in what used to be a toilet. Just rubbish bags and a hidden bowl.

I had no time to find the correct building. I went for it. A disused toilet block.

Relieved, I exited and then noticed the new toilet block – just 20 metres behind the abandoned building that I had stormed into. It was a demountable, relocatable building. I used it to wash my hands and try again.

Casually, I took my time to enjoy the walk back to the plane. As I did, I found myself wondering whether anyone had seen me storming into the wrong building and if I owed somebody an explanation or apology.

Back on board, I noticed that the man who'd been sitting in the single back-left seat had disembarked, so now I had the whole back row to myself.

After 15 to 20 minutes on the ground, we took off again. The next leg was 40 minutes. About 15 to 20 minutes in, the urge returned – worse than before.

I started weighing my options.

Just go for it and wet my pants? Hold on for another 40 minutes? Or…

I glanced around. No water bottles. But I did spot a sick bag. I thought to myself, *That would need to be waterproof to handle what it has been designed for.* It looked roomy enough for to handle the little I was managing to leak out each time. And right there in the seat pocket in front of me was one. Huh.

This was not ideal – but it was better than the alternative.

I leaned forward slightly, pretending to look out the window at the vastness of Serengeti. In truth, I was angling for comfort and privacy.

With my left hand holding the bag and my right making sure my aim was right, I managed it – no accident.

Three long minutes of amazing 'sightseeing'.

Relieved, I gently sealed the bag and tucked it into the seat-back pouch in front of me. No spillage. Mission complete.

If the pilots or passengers found out what happened in the back row, I'm not sure what they would have thought. Personally, I had just lived through one of the most bizarre and challenging moments of my life.

I can't imagine the absurdity of being the first person on this planet needing to resort to such a solution.

Maybe I was the first 61-year-old male… or maybe the first one to tell the story.

We were now over halfway to the next airstrip and, though I'd just relieved myself, I was already thinking about going again when we landed. This time, no animals on the runway. Smooth landing. A brief stop to collect the new passenger. I disembarked, found a proper toilet inside the small terminal and discreetly disposed of my sickbag.

It was now 36 hours in – midday – and I was standing at my third remote airport somewhere in the middle of the Serengeti. I couldn't describe it to you if I tried; I'd become hyper-focussed on one question: will I get the help I need?

Taking off again, I had a moment to look out the window. The opportunity to enjoy the Serengeti from a small plane is unreal – something I'd actually like to do again one day, with family and not preoccupied with pain.

The final leg – 35 minutes to Arusha. This time, I managed to hold on. The plane was now too full for privacy, so another in-flight sickbag stunt was definitely not an option.

We landed just before 1pm. I made a beeline to the terminal toilets – twice – once before picking up my bag and once after. The second time, I remember digging through my luggage for Panadol and Nurofen, trying to get ahead of the next wave of discomfort.

Outside, I found my driver from Zara Tours – a quiet man whose name I don't recall, but whose patience I'll never forget. He had been waiting for me for over two hours. Zamo had rung ahead before I left Seronera, based on the timing of the original flight plan. No one had known I'd be taking the scenic route.

I thanked him repeatedly as we jumped in the vehicle. Even with limited English, he knew he was my ambulance. He made a quick call to Zara Tours, speaking in Swahili and gave an estimated arrival time to be passed on to Dr Haggai, who was planning to meet me at Springlands Hotel after lunch. It would now be around 3pm, before we arrived there, thanks to the longer flight.

The drive from Arusha to Moshi normally takes about two hours, depending on traffic. We stopped three times for me to try and relieve pressure – fewer than I expected – which was a small mercy. One of those stops stands out. I couldn't find privacy and ended up relieving myself behind a building, fully exposed to anyone walking by.

Sure enough, a few pedestrians saw me – a lone white tourist behind a wall, taking a leak. They looked surprised. I didn't even blink. I was beyond embarrassment at this point.

Arriving at the hotel, Dr Haggai was already waiting. After a quick stop at the men's room – he pulled me aside to check in. Calm, professional, thoughtful – exactly what you want in a crisis.

He asked for a full update since I'd seen Dr Godwin, listened carefully and then told me to pack an overnight bag. "Just in case," he said. If a procedure was needed, we'd be ready.

Then we drove straight to the Moshi X-ray and Ultrasound Health Centre.

On the way to the centre, Dr Haggai gently prepared me for what might be ahead. First, we'd do an emergency ultrasound. Then, depending on the results, he had a local surgeon standing by, Dr Alfred.

The nurse was ready when we arrived. The scan confirmed it: my bladder was holding 740 millilitres of urine – about 50% more than the average capacity. Worse, my prostate had grown to around 125cc, up from 100cc just six months earlier. That made it more than three to four times the normal size, which is typically around 25 to 30cc, roughly the size of a walnut.

Dr Haggai nodded as we both stared at the screen. This confirmed Dr Godwin's diagnosis back at the lodge. The pressure from my enlarged prostate was blocking my urethra.

Unbelievably, despite the size and severity, I'd somehow still been able to pass a few drops every half hour for the past 40 hours.

Dr Haggai rang Dr Alfred with the results and asked him to meet us at his clinic in fifteen minutes. I'll never forget the last 100 metres of that drive. The dirt road felt like a theme park ride. I remember laughing through the pain as the car bounced its way to the entrance.

You couldn't script it.

As we pulled up, Dr Haggai explained the next step: they would attempt to insert a silicon catheter. If that didn't work, they'd have to go in through my abdomen and drain the bladder directly with a very different procedure. Through my stomach. No way. I'd rather take the pain through the preferred channel.

We entered the building – a simple, modest clinic with a few other patients inside. It was a far cry from what I was used to in Brisbane but none of that mattered. I was getting help.

A nurse set up an IV and gave me proper pain medication while we waited for Dr Alfred. About fifteen minutes later, he arrived, introduced himself, reviewed the scan and walked me through what was about to happen. Then he asked the question, "Michael, are you ready for us to give it a go?"

How do you answer that when you've never experienced what's coming? Again, I was out of options.

I took a breath, "Yes. Let's do it."

I was lying on a black metal-framed bed, a white sheet beneath me, legs steady. Dr Alfred got started. I was bracing for pain, steeling myself for the possibility that it might not work.

And then – before I could fully register what was happening – I felt a pressure release. Fluid started rushing through the tube and into the bag. The relief was instant. The pain stopped. Amazing.

In that moment, it was one of the greatest feelings of my life.

I didn't know how to celebrate the instant sweet release – laugh, shout, cry. It was an exhilaration.

My 40-hour ordeal – the pain, the burning sensation every time I tried to go – was finally over. It was a welcome change. But now, the focus had moved to the tube and bag attached to my body.

Dr Haggai picked up the bag and held it up for me to see.

"This is over a litre," he said – significantly more than the scan had shown. My bladder must've stretched quite a bit to cope.

Pretty incredible in itself!

That was a scary thought. Who knows what might have happened had I waited any longer – if I'd stayed on that safari vehicle instead of finding that airport. Things could have gone very differently for me.

As I lay there, pain-free for the first time in nearly two days, the conversation changed.

The doctors began discussing the next step. With the catheter in and doing its job, I'd be ok to return to Australia for surgery… with the catheter still in place! Excuse me?

I'd only just started relaxing and now my mind was racing again. As thoughts of how I would travel with the current set-up down below started, everything else hit me as well.

No Kilimanjaro climb. Not in two days' time. Not at all. Not this time!!!!

The change in thinking was almost too fast to process.

Dr Haggai explained that with the catheter, there was no need to keep me overnight. He'd take me back to the hotel where I'd be more comfortable. Just like that, we were on the move again.

When we arrived at the hotel, I stepped out with my overnight bag – and now a newly acquired plastic bag holding and hiding the urine bag. I was self-conscious, no question. The last thing I wanted was to draw attention to myself in the hotel courtyard.

I quickly figured out a system. Looping the tube, tucking it into my pocket, carrying the rest discreetly in the bags – I somehow got from the car to my room without raising eyebrows. No, I don't have a photo of that moment. Some things are best left to the imagination.

Back in the room, with a clear view of Kilimanjaro's snow-capped summit off to the right, I had a moment to take a deep breath. The mountain looked magnificent. Magnetic.

The Tanzanians say climbing Kilimanjaro is something you must do at least once in your life.

I didn't even take a photo.

I needed the solitude. It had been a huge day and I needed to regroup. I unpacked both bags; the one from the safari and the one I'd left at the hotel with all my mountain gear – another reminder of the now cancelled trip, the shattered dream.

I got to work figuring out how to operate with this catheter – not just lie in bed with it. The bag was a long rectangular shape; the tube measured at least a metre. It was awkward. I needed both hands free to work out how I was going to get around with this new appendage.

So, I had to get creative – time to put on my problem-solving cap. It took a bit of trial and error, but I eventually found a fix that worked.

The final solution was this: I looped the tube into three-and-a-half anti-clockwise circles and used a plastic hook – like a mini coat hanger – to latch the bag onto the waistband of my underwear. The bag hung down my right thigh, the coiled tube tucked neatly over the top. The whole setup perfectly concealed beneath my loose-fitting hiking shorts. I had succeeded. No bulges. No visible tubing. A had a fully functional, wearable solution. No need for the external bag I'd walked through the courtyard with.

This, I do have a photo of... though I'm not sure I want to show it (ha-ha).

MacGyver would've been proud. I realise I'm showing my age with that reference. For younger readers, MacGyver is an 80s TV show where the guy could build anything with a paperclip and a bit of chewing gum.

That night, I had my first shower with the catheter in. I used the hook to hang the bag from the cold tap – now I just had to avoid turning in circles and catching on something else. Funny what you notice when movement is no longer unrestricted.

Dinner was full of lovely choices, although I couldn't tell you what I ate. I was too chuffed to be walking around the dining area, catheter bag hidden, moving freely.

SHATTERED DREAMS & WEAKENED STREAMS

After dinner, I sent an email to my travel agent asking to bring my flights forward. Because of the time difference, I waited until morning to call the insurance company.

Later that night, I placed my new Bestie, the urine bag, on the empty side of the queen bed. It was a strangely welcome companion, and I slept through the night.

I honestly couldn't remember the last time that had happened. Maybe five years ago? Longer? Certainly, before I'd started seeing a urologist. Disrupted sleep had been my normal for a long, long time.

The next morning, after that glorious full night's sleep, I checked my email and saw more good news; my travel agent had managed to bring all my flights forward for a small fee. The first leg of my flight was now booked for the next evening.

This was excellent. It meant I'd be able to see Michelle and Anton off on their climb the next morning before beginning my own unexpected journey home.

Over breakfast, I realised I now had a full day to myself. A day to rest. Journal. Reflect. Call family. Maybe not swim – for obvious reasons – but at least catch my breath.

I rang my wife, Vicki, who had been holding the fort at home and keeping the family updated. WhatsApp messages were being sent whenever there was something new to report, but now and then, when possible, a proper call helped me talk things through. I kept Vicki fully in the loop and she did the same with the rest of the extended family. They helped me talk through my options and enabled me to stay focused on what mattered. I felt supported – even from across continents.

Later that morning, I had a visitor. Mama Zara.

Her reputation was well-earned. Respected and loved by her entire team at Zara Tours, she made a point of finding me personally. She already knew of my predicament. Word had spread. She greeted me warmly, then looked me in the eye and said, "I'm so sorry. I know you've come all this way to climb and now you have to go home."

I nodded, unsure of what to say.

Then she asked, "Michael, would you like to come back, after your operation and climb Kilimanjaro?"

"Yes," I said, without hesitation, "I'll be back."

With that, she did something extraordinary. She introduced me to Erasto, one of her senior managers and said, "Please provide Michael with a complimentary booking when he's ready to return."

We exchanged contact details. Erasto, ever the marketing mind, asked if I might bring a few people along for the climb. I told him I'd try, but no promises.

Michelle and I had tried months earlier to spread the word and get a bigger gang together for the climb. We thought four to six climbers would be ideal – not too many, not too few – but there had been no takers.

Back in my room, already pondering the return trip, one person kept coming to mind – a close friend I hadn't spoken to in years. Someone I'd hurt, deeply. We often used to talk about climbing Kilimanjaro together.

I wasn't ready to reach out just yet. But the thought stayed with me. Maybe in the new year, after the surgery, when training could begin again.

Meanwhile, in Brisbane, my wife had spoken to my urologist about my situation and need for immediate surgery. I was booked into the Brisbane Greenslopes Hospital, a ten-minute drive south of CBD, for Monday, the day after I due to land. Thanks to Vicki.

The insurance company had emailed to confirm that my condition met the criteria for early repatriation. I was cleared to fly. There was no urgent need for surgery in Tanzania, South Africa or Dubai. As long as the catheter stayed in and things remained stable, I could return home to Australia for treatment.

Late that afternoon, my brother-in-law, Anton arrived from Joburg (Johannesburg, South Africa). I waited until he'd checked in before catching up with him for a drink and a full debrief. Not long after, Michelle and Zamo returned from the final day of safari.

It was good to see them. Michelle and I hugged. There was relief all round – relief that I was okay. The disappointment was still there, of course. This wasn't what we'd planned. But we were honest about it. I gave them the good news... and the bad news. We took a deep breath together.

The mountain wasn't going anywhere – but for now, I needed help.

We planned to have dinner together and I joined them afterward for the traditional pre-climb briefing with Festo, our head guide.

Even though I wouldn't be joining the climb, I wanted to be there. I wanted to listen, take it all in – because I knew I'd be back. At one point during the session, I even found myself wondering whether it would be possible to summit *with* the catheter in. Ridiculous, I know. But I actually thought about it.

Michelle and Anton needed to focus now, after the briefing, so we said goodnight. There was gear to get ready, duffel bags to be packed and daypacks to be loaded.

The morning of the 6th of December arrived – the planned start date of the climb.

After a quick breakfast together, it was time for me to say goodbye.

I stood there as Michelle and Anton brought out their duffel bags and daypacks, loading them into the bus alongside the porters. This was the moment we'd all trained for, prepared for, dreamed about... and I wasn't going.

Watching the bus reverse out of the hotel car park without me on it was one of the hardest things I've done. I had trained for over six months to be on that bus. I stood there, holding back tears, managing a brave wave as they pulled away. It stung, for all three of us, in different ways.

Then I turned and walked back into the hotel.

I had my own bags to pack. Checkout was at 11am. My driver would arrive later in the afternoon to take me to the airport.

I found a relaxed spot in the hotel garden and sat down with my phone. I started Googling what it meant to travel internationally with a catheter and a urine bag. To my surprise, there was loads of information. More than I expected.

I discovered that I wasn't alone – not by a long shot. Many people had done this before me. In fact, some chose to travel this way by preference. You could empty the bag when it suited you, not when your bladder decided. No waiting for the required seatbelt sign to be turned off.

It was oddly reassuring. Thanks to Google, I no longer felt like the only person in the world flying long-haul with a catheter in a bag strapped to my thigh. Still, it didn't entirely take away the unknown of doing so.

Around 1pm, I went to the dining area to have lunch. There was plenty of time before the airport run.

And then, as I sat something happened that became one of the defining moments of the trip – and a key reason this book carries the title *Serengeti Serendipity*.

It's a phrase my sister came up with, after witnessing firsthand what I went through – and seeing how everything unfolded and fell into place. It just seemed too improbable to believe...

A man walked in, beaming. He looked like he was on top of the world.

I greeted him and asked, "What are you smiling about?"

"I just had a massage," he replied. "I summited Kilimanjaro yesterday and now I'm recovering."

He introduced himself. His name was, Mario. He was from Germany, and he spoke English well. I invited him to join me for lunch, and he accepted.

Everyone at Springlands Hotel was there to either climb Kilimanjaro or do a safari – or both. The place had a purposeful energy about it. Owned by Zara Tours, it felt like a base camp for adventure.

Mario had chosen to take on the mountain as a gift to himself for his 50th birthday.

Over lunch, I asked him all the obvious questions: How was it? What was the group size? How many days did you take? What would you do differently? What kind of energy bars did you take? How much water? Were you warm enough? Did you take altitude sickness tablets? Malaria meds?

He humoured me with thoughtful answers, and I mentally took notes.

Then the topic changed. Realizing I was from Australia, he asked if I'd ever been to Phillip Island – he was a huge motorsport fan, in particular Formula 1's. We didn't stay on that for long since I'm not exactly a motorsport buff.

I made a half-joking comment: "Sounds like you work for Formula 1 in Germany."

Mario smiled and said, "No – but I work at a hospital not far from a Formula 1 racetrack."

"Oh," I said. "What kind of work do you do at the hospital?"

"I'm a urologist."

What?! You're kidding me.

Suddenly, there I was – sitting at lunch, wearing a catheter and a concealed urine bag – being given an impromptu consultation by a German urologist who had just summited Kilimanjaro.

You can't make this stuff up.

Over the next 40 minutes, Mario walked me through everything. I shared my scan results, bloodwork, the Tanzanian doctors' notes, and my current condition. We both understood this was an informal chat – I'd be seeing my urologist back in Brisbane to confirm everything.

He explained, with both care and precision, the four types of operations available, along with the risks attached to each. Just contemplating them had me tensing up – hardly a bedtime story. He even told me which one he would recommend if I were admitted to his hospital.

"The robotic one," he said. "Your prostate is too large. It needs to be significantly downsized. With a history of benign enlargement, biopsies should be done during the procedure just to rule out any cancer."

Mario was an expressive man; he talked with his hands... a lot. He cupped them to show the prostate's shape, demonstrated the incision and then mimicked how the robot enters the centre, removes as much of the interior as possible and stiches the outer shell back together.

A three-hour operation. And exactly what I needed.

In that moment, I knew I was being looked after. For me, this was no mere coincidence.

We had a long lunch. Before I left to find my driver, we exchanged email addresses. I thanked him, shook his hand and walked out to the car.

Sitting in the vehicle, I was lost for words. Truly. In awe of what had just happened. As they say in Afrikaans – *Kan jy dit glo?* (Can you believe it?)

A urologist. From Germany. Fresh off the mountain. Joined me for lunch before I was due to fly home. Serendipity on steroids?

We pulled into Kilimanjaro International Airport late that afternoon. I took a deep breath. I was about to do something else for the first time – go through airport security with a catheter and a doctor's letter in my carry-on.

Despite all my Googling, my lunch with Mario, my phone call with the travel insurance company and the conversations my wife had with my urologist – there were still so many unknowns circling my mind, like planes waiting for clearance at a busy airport.

The first big question was this: What would the airport security scans reveal? Would they ask me to drop my pants and explain what I was hiding? I wasn't exactly smuggling diamonds – just a discreet medical plumbing arrangement, taped discreetly to my thigh. That doctor's letter had become my insurance policy – my way of saying, *"This is a medical emergency."*

Would they believe me? Would I make it back to Australia?

But then came the *bigger* questions: Could I get the operation I needed? Would it happen before Christmas? How long would I be walking around with a catheter strapped to my leg – trying to pass as "normal"? What if there were complications? I'd heard and read what could go wrong – and some of it wasn't pretty.

And what about the mountain? I'd said it. To Mama Zara and to Erasto, *"I will be back to climb Kilimanjaro."* But would I? When? And more importantly – who would come with me?

What I did know was this: **the mountain would have to wait.**

THE SPARK: WHEN THE MOUNTAIN CALLED

"It is not the mountain we conquer, but ourselves."

– Sir Edmund Hillary

CHAPTER TWO

❧

FROM ASHES TO ALTITUDE

W hy another adventure?

My 30th birthday, in December 1992, was a life-chang-ing moment. We were in Brisbane celebrating at my in-law's home in Brisbane. On the surface, it was a typical birthday gathering – good food, family, and friendly banter. But I remember it made me stop in my tracks and realise how little balance I had in my life. I was leading a pretty dull existence. I had no close friends that really knew one another, and I did no regular activities or sport. I was overweight. And there was not a single adventure in sight.

Over a decade earlier, in 1981, I had arrived in Australia on a Rotary Exchange year – and fell in love with an Australian. Something you're not supposed to do as an exchange student. But it changed everything for the better. A few years later, I left South Africa to marry Vicki and start our life together in Australia. I remember throwing myself into work, especially after landing a job with AMP as an insurance agent. I went all-in on this career track. But that was it. No sport, no hobbies, and no real outlet. Just the daily grind. Looking back, life had become narrow – pretty dull.

What really got me thinking about all this was the birthday cake.

Vicki had organised the party and invited the small group of people we knew as friends at the time. The cake was made by a work colleague of mine. It looked beautiful, decorated with a bright, sweet, mango icing. The thing is, I am not a fan of mangoes. Never have been. Can't really explain why, I just don't like them.

Of course, I ate some cake – I had to. But that mango icing hit me like a quiet truth: people didn't really know me. And more to the point, I hadn't put time and effort into being known. I wasn't consciously investing in friendships.

Surprisingly, while the mango cake was like a mis-spelled name on a birthday card – well-meaning but slightly awkward – it became a lasting gift of sorts. I enjoyed the cake, even though I left the icing and some-how, it gave me a much-needed wake-up call.

My birthday is close to Christmas. So, over the holiday period I had time to reflect, and the light really came on. I realised I'd completely let go of the team sports I used to play growing up in South Africa – rugby union, squash – and I had been more focused on work to make exer-cise a part of my life in Australia. No gym, no running, no squash. I had work and home – with my wife and two young children I dearly loved. But I'd lost a healthy life balance: quality family time, friendships, and community.

That wake-up call spurred changes in me. I started working on bringing balance back into my life – something I know always needs ongoing work. With hindsight now – and three decades later since my 30th – I'm grateful for the relationships I have, the sport I've picked up again, the exercise I enjoy, the new things I've tried and the adventures I've said yes to over the years.

Once adventures become part of your life, you start building a bucket list. And, for decades, Mount Kilimanjaro sat silently on mine.

The Inception of a Dream

I'm not exactly sure when I first heard about *The Roof of Africa* – Mount Kilimanjaro. Maybe it was in my twenties through Victor, my younger brother. He's the kind of guy who's a walking encyclopedia of African tourism – and just about everything else. Growing up, we didn't need Google. We had Victor.

I reckon it came up in one of those laid-back chats you have while enjoying a *braai* (well-known Afrikaans for 'barbecue' or 'grill'), when he would have casually mentioned this towering mountain in Tanzania – the highest in Africa and the tallest free-standing mountain in the world. However, it came up that little spark lodged itself somewhere in my mind. I didn't act on it at the time, but it never really left.

Years later, in my forties, the idea of actually climbing Kilimanjaro gained traction, largely thanks to a good friendship I had at the time. For about five years, we were involved in different ways with a non-profit organisation and even took a trip overseas for missions work. We were both drawn to adventure and would often talk about the Kilimanjaro climb as something we were going to do 'one day'.

Sadly, the friendship ended abruptly. Looking back, I can see how it might have been salvaged if I'd handled things differently. I still carry regret about that. There's a part of me that wonders whether unfinished dreams, like Kilimanjaro, gained more weight because of the loss of friendship that had once meant a great deal to me.

In fact, when I found myself back in my room at Springlands Hotel in Tanzania, after Erasto asked me to see who I could bring back with me, it was my old friend that came to mind. The mountain had once been *our* dream. I wasn't quite ready to reach out – but I knew that, in time, I'd try.

Kilimanjaro stayed on my mental bucket list, quietly waiting its turn while I tackled other adventures over the past two decades.

But life, of course, has a way of rearranging our timelines. Sometimes it's not an adventure that nudges us forward – but the passing of loved one that brings the family together, creating unexpected space for something new to emerge.

And in the togetherness, something stirs…

The Family Reunion in Mossel Bay

In August 2021, our father passed away. He was 79 and a half when he died from emphysema. Dad had a strong presence – charismatic, positive and always making the most of life, even after some wrong turns along the way.

He was gifted with his hands. If it was broken, he could fix almost anything – cars, furniture, leaking taps, toys. That was his way of showing love: through doing. He loved sport too – whether it was rugby, cricket, or squash, he appreciated the competition, the discipline and the camaraderie.

After a heart attack at 70, something altered. His faith became more a central part of his life. There was a softness in him in those later years – something deeply grounded. Dad wasn't perfect, but he owned his choices. He kept moving forward, kept smiling. And even when life knocked him down, he remained hopeful.

Like so many others during the COVID era, we weren't able to be with him in hospital. His phone had either gone missing, or the battery had died – we never really found out. That made it even harder. We couldn't speak to him directly. What we did know was that Dad died alone in hospital and we never had the chance to say goodbye. It was a silent kind of devastation.

With travel restrictions in place, a traditional funeral wasn't possible. So, we agreed as a family to have his body cremated and committed to honouring him further when the time was right. Our idea was simple but deeply meaningful: those who could make the trip would gather somewhere special in South Africa to scatter his ashes.

One of the silver linings of that COVID season was a new tradition we began in 2020 and maintain to this day: our fortnightly family Zoom calls. My wonderful mother – Ma to me (Mom to my siblings) – still keeps it running like clockwork, sending updates every six months to accommodate different time zones, daylight savings and the half-dozen countries we all now live in.

I mention this here because without those Zoom calls, I don't think the family reunion happened.

Over the course of six to nine months, between the regular Zoom catchups, we had occasional conversations about what to do with Dad's ashes. Eventually, we settled on a plan: a ten-day family reunion – from the 8th to the 18th of November 2022 – in Mossel Bay, near George in South Africa, where my youngest brother, also called Anton and his wife Geertje live with their three children.

Just a couple of hours up the "Garden Route" from there is a camping ground that holds a special place in our childhood memories – Ebb and Flow Rest Camp on the Touws River, near Wilderness. It's the kind of place woven into our childhood through old family photos – swims, braais, barefoot, fishing and warm nights under canvas. It was the perfect place to honour Dad, a location close enough for everyone, but meaningful enough to do justice to the moment.

Fifteen months after Dad's passing and after the small church funeral where more attended online than at the chapel service, about 40 all up, we finally did what we couldn't do in the days following his death; we came together. All six siblings and Ma. That, alone, felt like a small miracle. I counted 13 flights between the six of us just to make it happen. We gathered at Anton's home and spent ten days together. Early in the reunion, we made the drive out to the camping ground we'd frequented as kids, the place we had chosen to spread Dad's ashes

A Sacred Farewell – Dad's Ashes

On the morning of the 11th of November 2022, a lovely warm South African sunny day, we spread Dad's ashes in the river.

It was one of those rare, sacred moments life occasionally gifts you. We stood on a patch of grass by the river – nothing fancy, just a quiet, open space. A light breeze moved through, the kind you only really notice when you stop and take it in. Around us, life carried on – caravans, tents, families chatting, kids in the background. Across the water, a wall of reeds swayed gently. It was the perfect spot. Not dramatic, not staged. Just real. And it felt right.

I was about to say a few words when my brother Anton suggested we sit down on the grass before we began. And so, we did. We stayed there for hours – talking, laughing, crying. We shared stories; some light, some heavy, all important. It was healing in the truest sense of the word. Just that simple act of sitting down together opened the way for something deeply meaningful.

Afterwards, we went to a local restaurant for lunch and toasted Dad with the drinks he used to enjoy. My sister, Clare, reminded us of Dad's love for a beer shandy. Funny how everyone remembered something different. My sister, Emmy, carried plenty of memories; understandably so, given she and her husband my brother-in-law Anton had cared for Dad in his later years. My brother Anton, being the youngest sibling, didn't have clear memories of that old campsite, while Victor, Mr Google, no surprise, had plenty. That's the beauty of memory, it's not static. One person's recollection can trigger other memories, refresh forgotten ones and sometimes create new ones just by being shared aloud.

For the first time in a long while, we weren't just six siblings – we were a team. Like seasoned teammates stepping back onto the sports field; some of us older, even slower, but still playing for one another. We were carrying out something with Ma, each other and as a family for the man who fathered us. That day wasn't just a farewell. It was a reconnection – with each other, with our past and with something inside ourselves.

I remember feeling lighter after that day. A weight I didn't even fully realise I was carrying had been lifted. Maybe it was because I'm the eldest. Or maybe it was because I'd been the one to suggest cremation and that we wait until the world was free to travel again. So, that ee could be together in person to honour Dad. It had turned out to be pretty perfect. For whatever reason, it felt like something had lifted.

They say funerals are for the living, not for the dead – and it's true. A proper goodbye, when done well, doesn't just honour the person who's gone. It clears the space so that those still here can keep living. Fully. That's what that day gave us – the gift of moving forward, together.

I left that memorable day ready for a new chapter in life. I was ready to find something to look forward to. You could feel the shift taking place.

The Next Hike – Already Planned

Fortunately, my next hike was already locked in before the South Africa trip. The plan? A three-day adventure in December 2022 to Wilsons Promontory – the southernmost point of Australia's mainland – with a group of five tight-knit mates. We'd be hiking with full packs to the lighthouse. It was a solid goal to keep me moving and keep the life balance going.

The last big mountain challenge we took on was back in August 2020. The five of us had taken on Queensland's highest peak – Bartle Frere (1,622 metres). From the carpark, it's about a 15km return hike with roughly 1,000 metres of elevation. It's not for the faint-hearted – especially if you're doing it in one day, which we did. That meant an early morning start, pushing hard on the way up and a fast, slightly sketchy descent to beat the sunset. We made it – with sore muscles and a few close calls, but no injuries. Just that glorious kind of pain that reminds you that you're alive.

This group had been doing annual adventures like this since October 2011 – our first being the Auckland Half Marathon. We call ourselves the 'Elite Athletes' (EAs) – tongue firmly in cheek. If you check out our Facebook page, you'll see there's no arrogance in the name – just aspiration. Lately, we've joked about renaming it the 'Aging Elite Athletes', especially after recent, lower-key challenges; like five days of bareboat sailing around the Whitsundays in June 2023. Not exactly high-performance athletics, but a fantastic adventure all the same.

But just a few weeks before that planned hike – while I was still in South Africa – something unexpected happened. A different kind of spark was lit. I had no idea I'd be thinking about something much bigger before I even got to lace up for that three-day trek.

New Spark Emerges – Tackle Kilimanjaro

One afternoon during the reunion, after spreading Dad's ashes, we were sitting around my brother's lounge chatting. Someone – I can't remember who exactly, it might have been my sister Michelle – brought up the idea of climbing Mount Kilimanjaro. To our surprise, more than one of us had it on our bucket list.

Victor, naturally, had known about it long before the rest of us. He had shown interest on numerous occasions over the years. Michelle, though, wasn't just interested – she was ready. She leaned forward and said something that changed everything, "Let's go for it. Let's do some research after we get home and pick a date."

That simple sentence moved the idea from 'someday' to 'possibly soon'. And that energy, that shared sense of *maybe we could,* caught us all a bit off guard. It made it real. That moment was a welcome spark that set the whole climb in motion.

It's amazing how fear fades and courage grows, when you're not the only one saying yes. This is something I have come to realise – the EA group has quietly done for one another, time and time again. But this time, it wasn't the EAs. It was family – siblings, in-laws – talking about a possible adventure together.

I shared with Michelle and Victor that our brother-in-law Anton – my sister Emmy's husband – was keen as well. On my way over for the reunion, I met up with my sister Clare in Sydney. She lives in New Zealand with her family, and we flew together to South Africa. We'd stopped in Joburg for a few nights to see Emmy and Anton. One morning, as we enjoyed our coffees – still waking up – the subject of adventures came up. That's when I learned then that Anton had dreamed of climbing Kilimanjaro for years.

I always knew Anton had a serious adventurous streak. He'd run the 'Comrades Marathon' several times – a 90-kilometre ultramarathon between Durban and Pietermaritzburg. No joke. It's the kind of event where people cry crossing the finish line, not because they're emotional, but because they are in such pain with their legs cramping. So, Kilimanjaro wasn't just a vague maybe for him – it was unfinished business.

With both Anton and Michelle onboard, or at least leaning in, the conversation began to shift. It wasn't just an idea anymore. It was something that felt... possible.

The Spark Catches

That conversation did get us thinking – who else in the family might want to take on this mountain with us? More importantly if they could do so next year with us.

I think, deep down, most people who've done any kind of adventure know there's something special about doing it with others. It's not just about safety, or logistics, though these things matter. It's about the shared experience; the laughter, the encouragement when someone hits a wall, the inside jokes and those unspoken moments that forge real connection.

We're wired for belonging. And when a group sets out toward the same summit, something alters. It becomes more than a personal achievement; it turns into a collective story – one you can look back on and say, *"We did that. Together!"*

That instinct to include others, to bring them into something meaningful, was at the heart of our early Kilimanjaro conversations.

Inwardly, I was all in. I was leaning into the idea from the start. But I also know myself. I don't say yes lightly. I wanted to make sure I'd thought through everything before I committed. And I was also trying to be mindful of others around me, where they were at. I didn't want to derail the moment by over-talking it, or adding pressure.

But the truth was, I was excited. The idea of taking on something like this with the wider family lit something up in me.

Respecting Conversation Dynamics

These kinds of conversations aren't easy. As we sat around talking in Mossel Bay, the idea of climbing Kilimanjaro wasn't floated lightly. It wasn't just a pie-in-the-sky comment – it felt real. Bold. Worth doing.

But in moments like that, people rarely jump straight to 'yes'. There's usually pause. A kind of calm stillness. Each person slips into their own thoughts, sifting through a dozen unspoken questions:

- Am I physically up for this?
- What happens if I can't keep up?
- What if I don't make it – altitude sickness, injury?
- Can I handle being outside my comfort zone?
- What about the cold? The tents? The toilets?
- Can I take the time off work – and truly switch off?
- Will my family okay with me doing this?
- What's the cost – and can I actually afford it?
- Is this the kind of experience I really want?

You can sense that others are weighing up all the questions too, for themselves. No one wants to push too hard or too fast. These conversations aren't just about logistics – they're about giving each other space. Before anyone can commit, they need to feel at peace. Physically. Emotionally. Financially.

But when the idea is right and the timing clicks, something moves. You can feel it. The mood lifts. That's the beauty of dreaming in good company; a group of people, each silently wondering, *"Could I actually do this?"* And suddenly, the impossible starts to feel just a little bit more possible.

To help keep momentum going – without putting anyone on the spot – we agreed to take the next step: to start looking into it. No pressure, no immediate decisions. Just commit to learning more, like Michelle had wisely suggested. I mentioned that I'd be stopping over in Joburg on my way back to Australia and would speak again with Anton (my brother-in-law) there.

We agreed that after Christmas, we'd start sharing our research findings and ideas in the new year.

That was a great decision. There's a lot to learn about climbing Kilimanjaro before making an informed decision. Every year, thousands of adventurous souls attempt the summit of Africa's tallest peak – just shy of 6,000 metres above sea level. Recent estimates suggest that between 30,000 and 50,000 climbers take on Kilimanjaro annually, most during the seven-month dry season.

Supporting this wave of climbers are more than 200 local and international tour operators, each offering a variety of routes, packages and timelines tailored to different fitness levels, budgets and appetites for adventure.

Michelle offered to set up a WhatsApp group so we could all stay connected, share research and keep the fire alive. A simple action, but an important one.

By the time I left South Africa, it felt like more than an idea. We hadn't all said yes yet, but something had moved in our thinking. The mountain was calling. And out of that reunion, born from grief and reconnection, came the surprising possibility of finally climbing the world's highest free-standing mountain.

Testing Myself – Wilsons Promontory

Travelling home to Australia, it hit me – we were serious. We were actually talking about climbing Kilimanjaro.

Fortunately, before a firm decision was needed, I had the three-day hike coming up at Wilsons Promontory with the EA crew – a perfect chance to test myself. In hindsight, the timing couldn't have been better. It gave me a chance to see where I was really at – physically, mentally, emotionally. And as always, doing it alongside my EA friends made all the difference.

We were carrying 15kg backpacks, covering long distances each day and pushing ourselves just enough to wonder if we'd bitten off more than we could chew. It was tough, but good tough. And when it was over, we treated ourselves to a day at the hot springs south of Melbourne. Nothing makes a tired body, and sore legs feel better than a hot sauna.

More than the physical trial, the hike gave me something else – clarity. Like the early morning fog lifting on a morning trail ahead. It helped me see that I was wrestling with more than just fitness. I was weighing up the commitment Kilimanjaro would require. Was I really ready to lock in something that big? Did I want to get serious about my health, my training, my diet, my focus?

I know, if I am honest with myself, there was a part of me wondering if this was an opportunity – at 60 years of age – to prove something to myself.

The truth is, no matter how appealing an adventure sounds, it always demands something from you. Time. Energy. Intention. It's hard work – and we know it. That's the irony. For those with an adventurous spirit, it's not just the summit that calls us. It's the grind too. The training. The planning. The unknowns.

That's where the magic happens. It pulls you out of the everyday cycle of emails and to-do lists and gives you something real to chase. Something uncertain. Something hard. A goal you're not sure you can reach – and that's exactly what makes it worth aiming for.

Holiday Indulgence before Mindset Shift

I had the Christmas holidays ahead, and both of us were looking forward to a special family gathering and the usual great feast. Our children and their partners had travelled to Brisbane – Michelle and Rodrigo from Melbourne and Tim and Holly from the UK. Just as she had done for so many years, my wife spent days planning and creating a wonderful spread for the family to enjoy. Whether gathering the larger extended family or just the four (now six) of us, she has always spoiled us with a banquet – including the essential family recipe for rum balls, the Christmas fruit cake and the traditional plum pudding.

I know, I gave myself full permission to enjoy everything the festive season had to offer. The extra helpings. The desserts. The leftovers while watching the Boxing Day Test. Even the midnight bowl of ice cream, thanks to my benign enlarged prostate that had me up once or twice a night in those days.

Come the new year, I knew a decision was waiting to be voiced. One that if made would demand focus, energy, and would likely burn off any holiday indulgence I'd accumulated. And I was fine with that.

There's a time to let go and enjoy and a time to get disciplined. I was getting ready for the latter.

WhatsApp Group: The Next Stage

On 4th of December 2022, my sister Michelle, who lives near Amsterdam, created the 'Kilimanjaro WhatsApp Group', for the two of us and knowing we would add our brother-in-law Anton and my brother Victor and any other family if they said yes.

It was such a simple act, but it moved our thinking. That one message thread made it real. It created accountability. We weren't just talking about it anymore; we were starting to share. What had started as small spark during a family chat in Anton's lounge room, was now catching fire. The WhatsApp group was fuelling the flames.

Even though the group chat had been set-up before Christmas the sharing commenced; links to tour companies, comparing routes and trying to figure out the best time of year to go. Logistics. Costs. Altitude tips. Fitness plans. It was all there in that group chat.

I've always been a fan of WhatsApp groups. When they're used well, they're gold. They keep things moving – ideas, questions, updates, reminders. They help maintain momentum. Especially when you're spread across countries, time zones and different stages of life.

That group chat became our base camp, our mini-Mission Control, the place where we'd prepare for the real challenge – climbing Kilimanjaro.

Even though not fully committed, we were circling the idea. We were giving it shape. And the more we shared, the clearer it became.

We were getting ready to say 'yes' to the mountain.

None of us knew just how much that "yes" when we finally said it would come to mean.

The EAs – "Elite Athlete's" – A Decade of Adventures

What began as a tongue-in-cheek name for a group of five mates doing their first half marathon in 2011 has become the banner under which we have tackled adventures ever since. The name stuck, the performances didn't matter and the memories just kept coming.

🎯 **Reflecting on EAs Last Decade:**

- Dec 2010: EA concept born during a Christmas/New Year's chat
- Oct 2011: Auckland Half Marathon
- Aug 2013: Sunshine Coast Tough Mudder
- Aug 2013: 4WD Double Island Point trip
- May 2014: Tasmania – cycled Mt Wellington and climbed Cradle Mountain
- Mar 2015: Buggie Bolt 5km – Brisbane CBD run
- July 2015: Sydney City2Surf – 14km run
- Aug 2016: Queenstown skiing – The Remarkables and Coronet Peak
- Oct 2018: Camped on snowy Mt Kosciuszko – used snowshoes for first time
- Aug 2020: Cairns – Climb of Mt Bartle Frere (QLD's highest)
- Dec 2022: Wilsons Promontory Hike, Victoria – One night at lighthouse
- June 2023: Bare Sailing – 5 Days Whitsundays
- Nov 2024: Kooralbyn Weekend – Catch up and an easy Day Hike

🏔 **EAs Long-Term:**

Continue to find physical challenges for the five of us to take on and together have influence through charity work – currently the Ladybird Care Foundation.

🏔 Kilimanjaro – Quick Facts & Route Options

📍 Location: Tanzania, East Africa

✏️ Height: 5,895 metres (19,341 feet) above sea level

🔺 Type: World's tallest free-standing mountain (not part of a range)

📖 First Recorded Summit: 1889 by Hans Meyer and Ludwig Purtscheller

🧗 Climbers Annually: 30,000 to 50,000

✅ Success Rate: ~60-70% (depending on route and acclimatisation time)

📅 Best Time to Climb: Jan-Mar (quieter, possible snow at summit), and Jun-Oct (busier, clearer skies)

🕐 Average Trip Duration: 6-8 days

⚠️ Challenge: Altitude, not technical difficulty – 'pole' (slowly, slowly) is key.

🧭 Route Options:

- Marangu Route (🍵 'Coca-Cola Route'): Hut accommodation, 5-6 days, less scenic, and lower success rate.
- Machame Route ('Whiskey Route'): Most popular, 6-7 days, good acclimatisation, scenic.
- Lemosho Route: Scenic and less crowded, 7-8 days, high success rate.
- Shira Route: High-altitude start, similar to Lemosho, tougher start.
- Rongai Route: Northern approach, 6-7 days, drier and quieter, good for wet season.
- Northern Circuit Route: Longest route (8-9 days), circumnavigates mountain, high success rate.
- Umbwe Route: Steepest and shortest, very difficult, poor acclimatisation.

"The most effective way
to do it, is to do it."

– Amelia Earhart

CHAPTER THREE

✣

SAYING YES TO THE MOUNTAIN

The beginning of 2023 saw a sharp increase in the group chat activity – it was steadily buzzing. Bit by bit, we were growing in our understanding of what this adventure involved. Early on Michelle and I realised that we were already on the path to saying 'Yes' to the mountain. It was just a matter of time before we'd be fully committed.

With that awareness came the occasional check-in between us: When would be the best time to go? Who might want to come with us? Which company could we trust? What's the best route? How many days would we actually need on the mountain?

These weren't just casual conversations anymore. And that preparation, even in its earliest form, had momentum.

We were doing enough research to say yes – and to mean it.

There's something about that early stage of planning that feels light and exciting. You're not carrying a pack yet. Your boots are still clean. But the idea has found its way into your bloodstream, and you can feel the slow change happening from 'maybe one day' to 'we're actually going to do this'.

Making the Dream Known

One of our early conversations turned to the idea of growing the group. I can't say exactly when it came up, but I remember Michelle and I waiting to see if our brother and brother-in-law were going to join. That got us thinking… what would make for a good-sized group for something like this?

Somewhere between 'too small to share the load' and 'too big to manage around a mess table'. We figured four to six people, each known to at least one of us, would be ideal. Big enough for diversity. Small enough to stay close.

This wasn't about avoiding boredom with each other's company – far from it. Michelle and I had done plenty together over the years; snow skiing in Canada, spotting lions in South Africa, even running the New York Marathon back in 2004. We travel well together. We know how to laugh, how to handle stress, and when to shut up and just enjoy the view.

But this was different. This wasn't just another trip. It was a week-long *adventure*. The kind that tests you, humbles you, and changes you. And something about that felt worth sharing. The right group could multiply the meaning of it all.

Like assembling a team for a heist film – you want the right mix of skills, but not so many that the mess tent feels like an overcrowded hostel at high altitude.

So, we started spreading the word – not just with family, but now friends too. Slowly at first. A chat here, a coffee there. We let people know we were going. The reaction was mixed – curiosity, awe, excitement… and the occasional "You're doing what now?" But the more we shared, the more real it became.

That's when we realised, we needed to put a stake in the ground. A clear date. A defined route. A ballpark cost. People don't say yes to an idea as easily as they do to a plan. And if we wanted others to join, we had to give them something solid to lean into.

Information Night – Amsterdam

Michelle came across an event, an information evening about climbing Kilimanjaro hosted by a travel company in the Netherlands. She signed up straight away, even though it meant a ninety-minute drive for her to attend.

It turned out to be a well of information; practical, detailed and exactly what we needed.

It was held in a cosy room at a travel store, with eight people excluding presenters attending – most of them looking around the room silently sizing each other up. Some already had their sights on the summit, others were clearly just curious. Michelle reported a pleasant evening all round and said the presenters clearly knew what they were talking about.

Until then, most of our info had come from the usual places – Google, YouTube, TripAdvisor, and a few hiking blogs. Useful, yes, but disconnected – not the full picture. This was the first time a real person walked one of us through the whole experience start to finish.

That night changed things. It gave us the missing piece: clarity.

The presenter – a no-nonsense Dutchman – had climbed Kilimanjaro multiple times. He was practical, confident, not into fluff.

"This is not a holiday," he said early on. "This is an endurance hike. If you want luxury, go to Zanzibar." Fair enough.

He talked about the seven established routes – each one with its own personality. The Coca-Cola route, the Whiskey route, the scenic routes, the steep routes, the hush routes. The message was clear; the longer you're on the mountain, the better your body can adjust to the altitude – and the better your chances of reaching the top.

Michelle came away with a printed booklet in Dutch, packed with insights. That night she messaged me and said, "It has been rather informative – it filled the gaps." True. Things started clicking into place.

We learned that the dry months – June to October and December to February – were the ideal climbing seasons. December, surprisingly, was considered a 'shoulder period' – less crowded, cooler, but a lot more peaceful. Apparently, during peak months, over 250 people can attempt the summit in a single night. That's a lot of headlamps zigzagging up the same narrow trail. Not ideal.

The Climbing Dutchman also had this warning: on summit night, you leave base camp around midnight and climb for six to eight hours straight, in the dark with headlamps, cold and the air getting thinner. He told them to picture the mental fog, the dizziness, the urge to turn back. But then he said, "If you've trained, if your mindset is strong and if you remember why you came, you'll be fine."

In addition to the booklet Michelle took notes on everything; the gear essentials, the porter culture, altitude sickness tips, training prep, rest days, the *Diamox* debates, and the absolute non-negotiable, hydration. *Diamox*, we learned, was a little white tablet – more officially known as acetazolamide – taken to help the body acclimatise to altitude by stimulating breathing. Some swear by it. Others prefer to let the body adjust naturally. Either way, it was one of those topics everyone seemed to have an opinion on.

The phrase *'pole pole'* came up – a Swahili term meaning 'slowly, slowly'. Apparently, we'd be hearing it daily.

It wasn't all grim. There were tips about energy snacks, layering systems, what to pack in your daypack versus what goes with the porters. And at the end, a bit of optimism: "No one climbs this mountain alone. You'll have support every step of the way. And if you do the prep, Kilimanjaro will meet you halfway."

That line stuck with both of us.

Discovering Zara Tours

That same night, Michelle heard about Zara Tours. They were introduced by the organisation that hosted the information session, Camp Kilimanjaro Experience, as one of the most experienced operators on the mountain. No flashy presentation, just a reputation that spoke for itself.

What caught our attention was that Zara Tours took up to 10 percent of all climbers on the mountain each year. That's thousands of people trusting them with their once-in-a-lifetime shot at the summit. Not only did they know the terrain, but they also knew what it took to help people succeed. And just as importantly, they knew how to look after the people who might not.

Their website wasn't the slickest. However, the reviews told a different story; guides who inspired confidence, porters who went the extra mile, itineraries that allowed time to acclimatise properly and a history of getting people up and back safely. It wasn't long before Michelle and I were both thinking the same thing: *These are our people.*

They offered multiple route options. After going over everything Michelle had gathered, we landed on the Lemosho Route. It was longer and more scenic than most and known for its high summit success rate due to better acclimatisation. We also chose our window – mid-December. Just after the short rains, just before the big holiday crowds. A little colder, maybe. But less congested.

We didn't set out that day thinking we'd find the company that would take us to *The Roof of Africa*. But we did. And they would turn out to be a bigger part of the story than we ever imagined. It felt like everything was falling nicely into place.

Especially for me.

Two Became Three

After the information night, things started to move quickly.

Michelle and I agreed it was time to check in with the two people we most hoped would come with us – our brother Victor and brother-in-law Anton. Now that we had something concrete – a company, a route and a date – it was time to ask the question properly.

A few days later I called Anton.

"Hey Anton, are you busy?" I asked.

"What's up?"

"I've got specific details regarding Kilimanjaro for you to think about."

There was a pause. "This sounds like you guys are going for it."

"Ja boet (yes brother), we are – Michelle and I want you to join us in December. We're thinking the Lemosho Route. It's seven days on the mountain. A safari after. Can you commit?"

Another pause – longer this time.

"Give me the dates again and tell me more about the before and after?"

"Date is yet to be locked in with the company – but we are thinking early December. Are you in?"

I could hear the cogs turning. He wasn't saying no. I sent him the rest of the information and let him know about the safari plans. A few days later, he was in for the climb, but not the safari.

Michelle had a similar call with Victor. She told him about Zara Tours, the route we'd chosen and the plan to go just before Christmas. But his world was rather busy at the time. A lot going on. Home renovations. Big responsibilities. Uncertain timelines.

He didn't say no. To be honest he didn't want to. However, he couldn't commit.

That was hard. Especially because this had been something the three of us had separately dreamed of doing for decades. Still, life has a way of rerouting even the best intentions. We understood and respected his position, and we left the door open.

"If things change," we told him. "You can still join. You know where to find us."

It was bittersweet. But it was also a turning point.

By early March 2023, we emailed Zara Tours with a list of questions – gear hire, oxygen bottles, porter tips, adding people to the group later and the safari Michelle and I wanted to do after the climb. Within days, we had a detailed itinerary, a gear checklist and answers to everything.

We had a date, the 6th of December 2023, with a planned summit on the 10th of December.

Exactly 100 days after that initial "What if?" chat, three of us had officially said, "Yes to the mountain." It was happening.

The Power of Setting a Date

The three of us saying yes to the mountain meant we could confirm the dates with Zara Tours and something powerful happens the moment you lock in a date.

The swing is almost instant. One minute it's a dream, a 'someday' idea you throw around in conversation. The next, it's real. People start marking calendars. Weeks start getting counted backwards. Conversations changed from *if* to *when*.

And it changes you.

There's a strange magic in committing to something bold. Suddenly, your body gets the memo. Your brain starts problem-solving. Your routine starts bending to make space for the thing you've said yes to. It's no longer about talking – it's about preparing.

Setting a date for Kilimanjaro lit a fire under me. I started thinking in weeks instead of months. I mapped out hikes. I booked a doctor's appointment. I began testing gear. Even my diet altered slightly – I wasn't trying to reinvent myself, but I didn't want to be the guy dragging at altitude because I ignored the basics.

At 60, setting a big goal like this wasn't just about adventure, it was about *ownership*. It was choosing to step outside the predictable, to challenge the idea that your best moments have already happened.

And here's the thing; it didn't feel like pressure. It felt like momentum.

There's a big difference between drifting and aiming. Setting that date gave me direction. It forced clarity. It said, "This is real now. Let's get ready."

In retrospect, I think that was one of the greatest gifts of this whole journey – the way preparation brought additional purpose into the everyday. A goal like that wakes you up. It makes you want to rise to meet it.

It didn't just affect my weekends; it started to shape my weeks. I found myself monitoring my diet with more intention. I said 'no' to things that didn't serve the bigger 'yes'. I caught myself reading articles about altitude training at midnight. And, without meaning to, I became more present – at work, at home... everywhere. The mountain was months away, but it had already started changing how I showed up every day.

There's something about a goal that has a deadline. It cuts through the noise. It asks you to pay attention. I wasn't trying to become someone else – I was simply becoming more of the person I knew I could be. The kind who set challenge... and follows through.

Post-Climb Safari

In fact, we didn't just plan the climb. We planned the reward too.

We'd already decided: climb first, then a safari. But somewhere in all the research and back-and-forth with Zara Tours, we discovered they didn't just run climbs, they also offered safaris, treks, day trips and beach escapes. That made things a whole lot easier.

We had barely finished locking in the climb for the three of us, before Michele and I were scrolling through the safari options. It didn't take long to agree – we'd reward ourselves after the summit with a five-day safari. A way to rest, celebrate, and soak it all in.

The plan was simple: Climb Kilimanjaro, then trade hiking boots for binoculars and maybe spot the occasional elephant wandering across the Serengeti. After days of early starts, cold mornings, altitude headaches and slow plods uphill, we'd get to relax, sleep in a bed that didn't involve a mat, eat a proper meal and take a long exhale.

What could possibly go wrong?

There was something poetic about that rhythm – work hard, go deep, then rest and reflect. It felt right. We weren't just chasing the summit. We were giving ourselves time to let the whole experience land.

And let's be honest, if we went all that way to Tanzania, why not stay a little longer?

Michael, You Can Do It!

The feelings that followed after saying 'yes' were a mixed bag – equal parts excitement, nervousness, and, if I'm honest, a healthy dose of 'Oh crap'.

There was a definite buzz. I felt lighter. Energised. I was finally taking on something I'd talked about for decades. For the first time in a long while, I had something on the calendar that made me feel truly alive – something beyond the inbox and the to-do list. There was purpose in my stride.

But then, creeping in under the adrenaline, was the question I couldn't ignore: Can I actually do this? I was sixty. Not ancient, but also not thirty anymore. I had no idea how I'd handle the altitude, or whether my muscles would agree with me after day four. So, like any modern man having a midlife awakening, I turned to Google.

'How many people over 60 have climbed Kilimanjaro?'

The estimates were oddly comforting. Somewhere between 5 and 10 percent of climbers each year are over 60. The oldest male to summit was 88. The oldest female had been 89. Apparently, around 20 to 50 people over the age of 80 had made it to the top. That helped.

I wasn't trying to break a record. I just wanted to prove to myself that I still had it – that I could commit to something hard and see it through. To have the experience on my own terms and at my own pace.

That meant training. No way around it. And not just hiking or gym work – it meant proper medical check-ups too, to make sure there was nothing lurking beneath the surface. No shortcuts allowed.

Cue the 'oh crap' part... early alarms, disciplined weekends, digging out my hiking boots again, trying to remember what gear I already had.

I had to start thinking like someone preparing for altitude, not just heading out for another stroll around the block.

Soon my diary started to look like a training manual. I was popping magnesium tablets to keep the cramps at bay, and dealing with blisters as I started wearing my boots started working their way back in.

There's a paradox in this kind of goal. You crave the outcome – the summit photo, the bragging rights, the clarity that comes from doing something bold. But you hesitate at the cost. The commitment. The grind. And yet, weirdly, it's the grind that ends up being the best part. It gives shape to your days. It wakes you up.

I was ready. Time to lock in the discipline.

It had been almost three months since the EA group tackled Wilsons Promontory and now it was time for me to dive into every possible hiking trail in the southeast corner of Queensland. I found myself studying the 'Best Trails' app, scrolling through maps and checking out Brisbane well known Mt Coot-tha with all its well-used walking tracks on the Brisbane City Council website. It's amazing what's available these days compared to what we used to have forty-five years ago in the South African Boy Scouts. Back then planning a hike meant spreading out contour paper maps on the table, ringing locals, or someone's dad, for tips. Now, it's all at your fingertips – and I was making good use of it.

On second thoughts, I realised that I was "preparing" for the mountain long before I started officially training physically. Those 100 days leading up to the commitment saw me slowly chipping away at my doubts. I wasn't building fitness; I was building belief.

I needed to believe I could do it before I could take the first real step.

Nine Months to Be Ready

With the date locked in and three of us fully committed, the countdown officially began.

We kept spreading the word, hoping maybe one or two more adventurous souls would join us. The WhatsApp group changed gears. No longer just a place to float ideas, it became a space for progress. We started posting about weekend hikes, swapping gear advice, asking travel questions and comparing doctor check-ups. Even small things, like someone getting a new backpack, sparked conversation.

There was a sense of community now. We were in this together.

Nine months. That was our window.

Nine months to train, to prepare, to visualise ourselves on that mountain.

Nine months to become the kind of people who could meet Kilimanjaro with open eyes, steady breath and strong legs.

The mountain was calling – and we had answered with a 'Yes.'

- 🌀 *"Pole Pole"* all the way – slow and steady is not just advice, it's survival.
- 📱 Tip: Longer route = better acclimatisation, fewer headaches, and higher summit success rate.
- ☁ December is a shoulder month – cooler, quieter, with clearer views and fewer crowds.

SIDEBAR: Seven Days on the Lemosho Route – Day by Day Breakdown

📖 **The scenic and steady path to *The Roof of Africa***

Day 1 – Londorossi Gate to Mt Mkubwa Camp (Big Tree Camp)
– Starting altitude: ~2,100m
– Short hike through lush rainforest. First glimpse of altitude.

Day 2 – Mt Mkubwa to Shira 1 Camp
– Enter the heather and moorland zone
– Scenic views, gradual ascent to ~3,500m

Day 3 – Shira 1 to Shira 2 Camp
– Easy acclimatisation day on the plateau
– Often used for slow gain and adapting

Day 4 – Shira 2 to Barranco Camp (via Lava Tower)
– Acclimatisation highlight
– Hike up to Lava Tower (~4,630m), then stop to sleep lower at Barranco (~3,960m)
– 'Climb high, sleep low' strategy

Day 5 – Barranco to Karanga Camp
– Scramble up the Barranco Wall
– Shorter day, helps rest and recover

Day 6 – Karanga to Barafu Base Camp
– Final base camp (~4,673m) before summit
– Early dinner and early sleep before summit push at midnight

Day 7 – SUMMIT: Barafu to Uhuru Peak (5,895m), then descent to Mweka Camp
– Midnight start
– 6-8 hours to the top
– Long descent after sunrise to much lower altitude

"Adventure isn't hanging off a rope on the side of a mountain. Adventure is an attitude."

– Chris Bonington

CHAPTER FOUR

❧

GOING ALL IN, COMMITTED

Fully committed – I was all in.

Nine months felt like a comfortable stretch of time to be ready, I knew it would fly by. This wasn't just about getting fit; it was about building a routine I could stick to, ticking off medical clearances, gathering gear, sorting travel, and seeing if I could squeeze in some altitude training – and most importantly, getting my head in the right space.

The Hiking Dutchman had made it clear: we'd need at least three solid months of proper training to be ready. But I knew this was about more than fitness. It was personal. Medical. Mental. Spiritual.

I wasn't becoming a mountaineer in the technical sense – no ropes or ice axes – but I was training for altitude. Training for resolve. I was becoming an **altitude climber**, preparing for thin air, slow progress, the *'pole pole'* pace we'd been told about and unpredictable conditions.

And I was determined not to leave anything to chance.

Training Together – Three Continents, One Goal

Anton, Michelle and I began sharing our individual plans in the WhatsApp group – ideas for training and how we were going to take on the coming months. Despite being spread across three countries and continents, we managed to build accountability into our routines. Anton and I were heading into winter, while Michelle was entering the European summer. Unlike Joburg or Brisbane, Amsterdam had no mountains, so Michelle had to get creative; tall Amsterdam Centrum buildings with stair access, steppers at the gym and regular walks around the city.

Anton kept running – something he genuinely enjoys – while also adding long walks and the occasional mountain hike. No gym work for him. We each found our own rhythm.

After reading up on what other climbers had done to prepare and figuring out what would work best for me, I put together a weekly training schedule that looked something like this:

- **Walking during the week** – Runners on and mileage under the feet. I steadily increased both time and distance, building consistency.
- **Weekend hiking** – Boots, two pairs of socks, a daypack, a CamelBak loaded with 4-5 kilos (mostly water) and off to the trails. Allowing for travel and time, I reckon over about eight months I easily logged 80 to 100 hours hiking in Southeast Queensland – some familiar places, some new discoveries. Still, I've probably seen less than half of what this beautiful part of the world has to offer.

- **Swimming two to three times a week** – Since running now triggered pins and needles in my arms and hands (a lingering effect from a 10km obstacle challenge – neck injury in 2013), I took up swimming to increase fitness. I found myself struggling to experience buoyancy. My backside was dragging well and truly below the surface. Swimming fast seemed to help, but it was not something I could do for one kilometre (20 laps). Maybe, only six laps, and that was with regular stops. After watching YouTube tutorials, I learned I wasn't breathing correctly. Once I figured out how to use my diaphragm, it all changed. I gradually built up to the twenty laps – not always gracefully – but enough to call myself a swimmer.
- **Squash (until three months out)** – I've played fixtures for decades since the wake-up call at my 30th birthday. But squash has a way of producing sudden injuries and I wasn't taking chances this close to the climb. Oddly, no pins and needles while playing squash, but I made the smart call to pause.
- **Gym work** – Once squash was shelved, I added gym workouts. My legs were strong from all the years of squash and recent hiking, but I wanted upper-body strength. Swimming helped, but the gym gave me that extra edge. That said, I think I spent more time in the sauna than on the weights' floor. Balance, right?

It wasn't until after Easter that I was consistently training four times a week. Thankfully, I had time to ramp up gradually – fitting in the regular training alongside the medical check-ups and two unexpected operations that followed.

Health & Check-Ups – No Stones Unturned

One of the real gifts from my years with the Elite Athletes group has been the open conversation about men's health. We've normalised things like annual check-ups, talking about test results and asking questions about our bodies. We've encouraged each other to see our GPs, to do the annual check-ups and see cardiologists, urologists, etc – whatever is needed.

The key here is a proactive approach to our health. We're not waiting for something to go wrong – were getting ahead of it. The mindset has also earned us the gratitude of our families. When we invest in our health, it's not just for our own benefit. We've all seen those ads where a child asks Dad to give up something – and it hits home.

History is full of actual elite athletes who've spoken openly about the importance of looking after their physical and mental health – not just for performance, but for the people around them. When we take care of ourselves, we lift the load for our families too. That's what peace of mind looks like – it's not just personal, it's shared.

Grateful for the influence of my mates, I booked early in the year to see my GP and explained I was aiming to climb Kilimanjaro in December. I wanted to be sure this 60-year-old frame was up for the task. He ran the full service; blood pressure, weight, blood tests and referrals to an ENT, cardiologist and urologist.

Expected results: I needed to lose 5kg (more would be nice) and monitor my cholesterol.

Unexpected results: I needed two operations. Yup. Two.

The ENT referral was driven by a simple question – was I breathing properly through my nose? One evening in the kitchen, Vicki made a passing comment about my heavy breathing. It made me notice…

Turns out my nasal turbinates – the 'air-con' of the nose – were enlarged, reducing airflow. And, with Kilimanjaro on the horizon, that made the decision easy. Better airflow meant better oxygen uptake at altitude. It was a no-brainer. Surgery downsized the 'air-con' at the back of my nose and I noticed the difference immediately. Amazing what we get used to over time.

The second operation came after I noticed something odd during sit-ups. Yes, I was doing sit-ups at the gym. Another GP visit led to a referral, then a surprise diagnosis: hernias. Not one, not two, but three. I had to choose; operate now or wait until after the climb. Recovery would take two to three weeks. I opted to go for it and managed the downtime with adjusted training.

The operations ended up being good for life, not just for the big mountain ahead of me.

A Small Pharmacy

By this point, my medical prep was starting to spill beyond appointments and scans – it was turning into a checklist of what to pack and how to stay ahead of anything that might go wrong on the mountain. Conversations in our WhatsApp group, advice from my brother-in-law's GP, and a few YouTube rabbit holes led to more questions.

Should I take iron supplements? Get a yellow fever jab? What about malaria tablets? Diamox for altitude sickness? I took all of my questions to my GP.

Closer to departure, about a month out, I popped into my local chemist to pick up iron tablets and a few other things. He'd seen me a few times by then and knew what I was gearing up for. As he looked over the script, he smiled and asked the kind of rhetorical question only a pharmacist can get away with, "Is there anything you haven't thought of?"

I laughed. Honestly? At that point, I couldn't think of much. Between the GP, the cardiologist, the urologist, two operations, a vaccine checklist and a growing pile of pills, I felt like I'd covered every base. Every known base, at least.

By then, I'd done a stress echo and got the all-clear from my cardiologist, had my annual urologist check-up (good to climb), recovered from two surgeries and was now ready to travel with a small pharmacy. All of this gave me the real quiet confidence that I'd done everything I could to prepare. And that helped my mindset enormously.

Fitting In Altitude Training

As part of my research, I learned that spending time at high altitude – specifically above 1800 metres – stimulates the body to produce more red blood cells – crucial for oxygen transport above 5,000 metres. This happens through a natural hormone called EPO (erythropoietin), which triggers your bone marrow to increase red cell production. But those extra cells start disappearing after about 30 days if you don't stay at altitude. Therefore, timing was everything.

I needed a pre-Kilimanjaro altitude hike.

I explored options for altitude time. The Drakensberg in South Africa, the Aberdare Range in Kenya, the Swiss Alps, the Himalayas in Nepal and the Hajar Mountains in Oman. Each location had its pros and cons. In the end, I chose Oman – remote, rugged and home to Jebel Shams, the highest peak in the country at 3,009 metres. My ever-helpful travel agent, Joe, let me know Oman Air was running a great promotion at the time, which helped make the decision. The plan was set. Less than two weeks out from the 6th of December, I would go via Oman, spend ten days at a higher altitude, summit Jebel Shams and give myself the best chance of preparing my body for what was to come on Kilimanjaro.

Remember the quote from Sir Edmund Hillary about conquering ourselves, not the mountain? The truth here stayed with me. As I mapped out my Oman trip, it echoed in the background. I wasn't trying to conquer Kilimanjaro. I was preparing for the internal climb – the one that starts long before you set foot on the mountain. Spending time at higher altitude wasn't just about building red blood cells – again, it was about building belief. I needed to know I could do it. And that meant getting my head there long before my feet could follow.

Locked-In Travel – The Itinerary

I'm not sure what came first – discovering the hiking option in Oman or scoring Business Class flights with Oman Air. Either way, some comfort before sleeping on the mountain, on a one-inch mattress for six nights, sounded good.

Here's how the final schedule ended up being:

- **16 Nov 2023** – Flight Brisbane to Sydney.
- **17 Nov** – Flight Sydney to Muscat, Oman (via Thailand).
- **18-20 Nov** – Dubai, UAE: be at the final day, Sunday 19 Nov, DP World Golf Tournament.
  Yes, I love following the players on the golf course – though I am not good enough to really enjoy playing the sport myself.
- **20-28 Nov** – Oman: Hajar Mountains for altitude time.
- **28 Nov** – Flight Muscat to Dar es Salaam, Tanzania (overnight).
- **30 Nov 2023** – Flight in Tanzania, Dar es Salaam, to KIA Kilimanjaro: Springlands Hotel, Moshi, owned by Zara Tours.

- **1-5 Dec 2023** – Safari: Elephant Park, Ngorongoro and Serengeti with Zara Tours.

As already explained, we'd originally planned to do the safari *after* the climb, as a bit of a reward. But looking at the flights it would've meant arriving home the week of Christmas and that felt too tight. Not enough time to cope with jet lag and still be present for all the Christmas matters. I wanted a few days to decompress – not go straight from the airport into holiday mode. So, I asked Michelle if could flip the schedule: safari first, then the mountain. A simple logistical decision – but in hindsight, a fortuitous one.

- **5 Dec** – Return to Moshi; Anton arrives from Joburg
- **5 Dec (evening)** – Kilimanjaro brief with Festo, our lead guide
- **6-12 Dec 2023** – Kilimanjaro climb: summit on 10 Dec 2023
- **13 Dec** – Depart Tanzania; return to Brisbane.

Packing – More Than Just Gear

With the flights locked in, it was time to turn my attention to what I'd be carrying.

I'm happy to admit that, for most of my travels, I've packed the night before, or even the morning of the flight departure, especially if the flight is later in the day. I like that. Yes, it's true, that I've arrived at a travel destination only to discover I'd forgotten to pack something as result of this routine. One memorable 'something' was underpants! It's become a bit of a game; can I get through the trip without needing to buy something I did not pack?

But this time was different. There's no shop at 4,000 metres. What you pack is what you live with – for seven days, at altitude, with no room for oversight. So, contrary to my usual style, I laid everything out about four weeks beforehand and started looking for flaws.

I went through the Zara Tours gear checklist and made some calls about what I'd bring versus hire. For example, I opted not to take a sleeping bag. Zara hires out minus 15-degree bags and the idea of saving space and less weight to travel with made perfect sense. I could rent one directly through them and it would be ready and waiting when I arrived. The WhatsApp group was useful again – we chatted through gear options, layering strategies and brands.

My packing system had categories:

- **Day Pack** (CamelBak) – In addition to the day's hiking gear – boots, trousers or shorts, shirt and watch – I carried 3 litres of water (a CamelBak and two bottles), poncho or raincoat, snacks, tablets, sunscreen and an extra warm layer.
- **Duffel Bag** – Max weight: 15kg. Carried by porters in a giant black waterproof bag. This held all gear for the seven-day hike. At each camp, your bag would be waiting in your tent – ready for the next day's prep and overnight recovery.
- **Travel Essentials** – Passport, tourist visa (easy to acquire), yellow fever certificate, flight details and travel insurance. I personally used the travel insurance provided through my credit card.
- **Non-Mountain Stuff** – Laptop, extra clothes, toiletries and anything else not needed on the mountain went into secure storage at Springlands Hotel. For a small fee, they also offered small lockboxes for passports, jewellery and cash – very helpful.

More than ever, the WhatsApp group proved to be the heartbeat of our operation. It wasn't just about training updates anymore; it was where we swapped packing lists, shared articles, tips, and fired off count-down messages as the days ticked by.

Michelle could ask a question while I was asleep in Brisbane, and I'd wake up to it. Anton would send a training clip from Joburg, and we'd all see it by lunch. No schedule needed – it just flowed naturally.

We only had two Zoom calls; one right after Michelle's info night in the Netherlands to consolidate learnings and one about three months out to finalise travel logistics and gear. Two calls – that's all. The WhatsApp group did the rest. It kept us linked, motivated and moving forward.

On the Zoom call about three months out, we acknowledged we hadn't been able to grow the group as we'd hoped. It was going to be just the three of us, supported by a local crew of about ten porters (roughly three per climber), plus chef and a lead guide. Still, we stayed positive and encouraging. No complaints. Just strong silent resolve.

Three people. Three continents. One mountain. Poetic, in a way.

Mindset – The Quiet Work

Alongside all the outward preparation, there was something going on under the surface.

It's amazing that there's so little talk about 'mindset training' when people prepare for something like Kilimanjaro. We naturally focus on the physical stuff – gear, health checks, flights, training plans. But you're thinking matters just as much.

From the day you decide to go for it, the climb begins – inside you.

I found that over those nine months, a bunch of little things chipped away at doubts and built belief. YouTube videos showing people, just like me, making the summit. Gear tutorials that made the logistics feel less overwhelming. Route reviews that helped me picture what each day would be like. I was absorbing not just information, but confidence.

Exactly. This wasn't just about whether my legs could handle the hike – it was about the mental resilience to keep going when it got hard, wet, cold, slow, or silent. Sometimes, the most powerful motivators come from unexpected places.

One of the most moving items was a news' article my mother Googled and sent us a few weeks before the climb. It told the story of three prisoners of war who escaped from a British camp in Kenya during World War 2 – just so they could try to summit Mount Kenya, Africa's second highest peak. They had almost no proper gear, no team support, little experience – yet they made it most of the way, planting a flag just short of the summit. It lit something in me. I realised, it was a stark contrast to how privileged we were. We had time, gear and a full team. If the POWs could do it, we could do this too.

I also spent time studying the daily distances and elevation changes. It was reassuring to compare these stats to my hikes around Southeast Queensland. Often, I was doing similar distances – just at a faster pace, which meant I'd likely be fine with the slower, altitude-adjusted trek. That gave me something solid to hold onto when the nerves crept in.

One of the bigger realisations for me – something I've touched on already and keep coming back to – is that mindset work is part of why I like saying yes to things like this in the first place. The adventurous spirit doesn't just crave the view; it craves the stretch – the challenge that forces you to examine your thinking and grow through it.

There's one quote that comes to mind. It captures what it really means to take on a challenge:

> *"The only limit to our realization of*
> *tomorrow is our doubts of today."*
> – Franklin D. Roosevelt

Yes, there are others, but this one has stuck with me. It helps me pause and ask: *What am I doubting right now?*

It does capture something I've come to believe deeply; that mindset isn't just part of the journey; it is the journey. Each small shift in thinking helps unlock something new and before you know it, you're doing things you once thought were out of reach.

Altitude – High Enough

I say, 'altitude time', not 'altitude training', for a reason. I wasn't trying to break a record, or train like an elite athlete. I simply wanted to spend time up high so my body could adapt and start building those red blood cells, boosting oxygen delivery before the real climb began.

The plan unfolded beautifully. I landed in Muscat, hired a car and drove to Dubai for a few days of world-class golf – watching, not playing. After that, it was back to Oman for nine nights of altitude time. I booked a series of inexpensive short stays through Airbnb – two to three nights at a time – basing myself at around 2,200 metres. The goal was simple: spend as much time as I could outdoors, hiking, climbing, moving.

The big one was Jebel Shams, the highest mountain in Oman at 3,009 metres. The climb took six hours up and four hours down – long, steep, rocky, with trails that punished the legs. I came down in the dark, guided by a headlamp, picking my way over sharp stones in the moonlight.

And then, one of those moments you just can't plan...

As I reached the base, I stumbled upon a group of Omani locals having a barbecue in a dry riverbed. They saw me emerge from the shadows, headlamp on, dust-covered and tired. With warm smiles and broken English, they waved me over. Before I knew it, I was sitting with them, sharing food, trading stories, laughing under the stars.

We passed around a pot of tea and a bag with dates – as it is the tradition in Oman. Sweet, sticky and connecting. It was the perfect end to a hard climb.

It reminded me of growing up in South Africa – of the unspoken rule that if there's a braai going, you're welcome. It's how we get to know our neighbours.

The next morning, I braced myself for sore legs, maybe even some lactic acid. But there was almost nothing. A bit of tightness, but no stiffness, no pain. I took some magnesium tablets, just in case the cramps showed up later.

That's when it hit me – something had shifted. Not just physically. Emotionally, I felt ready for Kilimanjaro.

The Final Stretch – To Tanzania

On the 28th of November, I flew from Muscat to Dar es Salaam, Tanzania, for the first time. I had a one-night stopover there before catching the morning flight to Kilimanjaro International Airport, the closest airport to Moshi. By then, my stomach had started to play up. On a quick call with my wife, I mentioned what was going on, wondering aloud if it might be the malaria tablets – I'd only just started taking them and I'd heard some people react badly.

Vicki listened, asked a few questions about the symptoms and gently suggested it might be food poisoning instead. "Did you take the charcoal tablets?" she asked. She always prepares well for travel especially with items for potential heath emergencies. Thankfully, this time they were part of my small pharmacy – I'd packed days before too, for once. Thinking back, it could well have been that meat platter I enjoyed in Muscat the night before I flew out.

At that point, I wasn't sure what to blame. I took the tablets, drank heaps of water and hoped it would pass quickly.

The morning flight from Dar es Salaam to Kilimanjaro took just over an hour. It was a clear day and not long after the crew made the usual announcements about descent and seatbelts, the pilot came over the intercom with something different. He told us to look out the right-hand side of the plane for our first glimpse of the mountain.

Wow! Absolutely majestic!

I happened to be on the right-hand side. There it was – Kilimanjaro – rising above the clouds, commanding respect. With hardly any cloud cover, I had an uninterrupted view of the mountain. A blanket of snow clung to the summit, and its size was staggering. No wonder they call it *The Roof of Africa*. You could see why it would take us days to climb. You can read about it, hear about it, train for it – but seeing it for the first time… that hits differently.

The Mind Games

Seeing the enormity of the mountain, I found myself having to manage my thoughts again. Big time. As I have already shared, the mental game never really stops – you're dealing with wondering if you can do it.

You don't climb a mountain like Kilimanjaro to only conquer it – you climb it to conquer yourself.

Yes, suddenly your mind starts to go to work. The doubts start to rush in. Thankfully, I'd done the prep – not just physical, but mentally. I was ready for these moments of awe and fear.

Still, I remember exactly what popped into my head, one after the other:

- *I'm about to try and climb a mountain that sits at the same height this plane is flying over 20,000 feet. And this plane is pressurised. I'm going to be walking up there without any of that help.*
- *That's a lot of snow on the summit. Am I going to be warm enough? Should I have hired extra gear?*
- *No wonder it takes days to reach the top. Maybe we should've signed up for the eight-day climb instead.*
- *This isn't some weekend adventure. Seven days in a row. No recovery time. No magnesium baths. No spas. No massages.*
- *What was I thinking?*

But then the counter-thoughts arrived. The stuff I'd stored up. The stories. The stats. The people I'd spoken to. I reminded myself: *Michael you're not the first.*

This mountain has magnetism. It pulls people in. Year after year, they come from every corner of the world for one reason – just to stand at that summit.

Many had gone before. Many would go after.

And now… it was my turn.

And I was about to give it my shot.

The Adventure I Love – This is it!

That whole season – nine months of buildup – was the kind of adventure I love. The grind. The structure. The soreness. The swimming. The check-ups. The WhatsApp banter. The altitude time. The magnesium tablets. The early nights and the good sleep.

The quiet, relentless discipline of preparing for something that might still break you.

There's a kind of thrill in working toward something with no guarantee. A summit you might not reach. An unknown you can't control.

But that's the point.

This chapter wasn't just about Kilimanjaro. It was about what happens when you go all in – when you train, prepare, trust and hope. When you do the hard work, knowing it might still not be enough.

I knew I'd done the hard work to give myself the best possible shot.

And now… it was time to climb the mountain.

SECTION TWO

THE SETBACK: WHEN THE BODY SAID NO

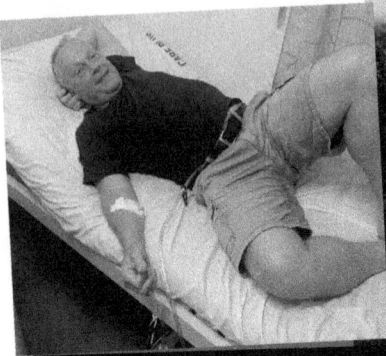

CHAPTER FIVE

GROUNDED IN THE SERENGETI

Touchdown in Tanzania – my first time.

I had just over a week to go before the climb – eight days, to be precise and I felt good… food poisoning aside. The altitude *'time'* had gone well, I'd pulled up fine after the ten-hour climb up Oman's highest peak, so I felt ready...

Whether my body had actually produced more red blood cells, I couldn't say – I was relying on science. With the summit planned for sunrise on the 10th of December 2023, I hoped science would prove true.

The climb was due to start on the 6th of December, so I had time to shake off the lingering food poisoning. I decided I'd wait until I reached Moshi before seeing a doctor – unless things got worse. In the meantime, I'd already switched to the BRAT approach bananas, rice, applesauce, and toast. Thankfully, I like all of them – especially bananas on toast – so it wasn't a difficult change.

I couldn't be sure whether the malaria tablets were making things worse. I'd started taking them a few days earlier, as prescribed. My main issue was diarrhoea, I wasn't experiencing the other usual red-flag side effects, which you get warned about with Lariam (Mefloquine) – things like nausea, vomiting, or dizziness. Still, there was stomach pain, a low-grade fever and some persistent headaches. My gut – figuratively and literally – was telling me to stop taking the Malaria pills, but I also decided to wait until I could speak with a doctor.

Moshi – Springlands Hotel

Zara Tours had a driver waiting at the airport with my name on a clipboard. It was a good time of day to be on the African bitumen roads and the drive to Moshi took only about 40 minutes. We were headed to Springlands Hotel, booked though Zara Tours. Somewhere along the way, we stopped so I could get a photo with the mountain in the background – a photo, I still treasure. It reminds me of a time when I was on the edge of something big, staring down a challenge I had no idea whether I could conquer… even though the actual challenge wouldn't involve the mountain this time.

Trying to remember what you wrestled with before doing something hard is tricky once it's behind you. Once you've succeeded, you know the outcome – and it's difficult to unknow something once it's known.

When I arrived at the hotel, I had no idea I was about to face my biggest health challenge, just two days later. I was feeling confident. The food poisoning hadn't gotten worse, and the BRAT diet seemed to be working.

Wanting to play it safe, I went to reception and asked for help to see a doctor.

To my surprise, they told me the doctor would come to the hotel.
A house call. In the middle of Africa!

What a luxury!

Dr Haggai has built a clever working relationship with local travel companies to care for tourist needing medical help. As part of his setup, he offers in-room consultations – yes, actual house calls to the hotels where travellers are staying.

That's how I ended up with an appointment before lunch.

When Dr Haggai met me at the hotel, I had no idea we'd end up becoming friends – or that I'd be seeing a lot more of him just later in that week. We chatted about a few things, including how he got his first name – his mother had named him after the Prophet – and how "Michael" isn't actually my first name. It's Ockert, my dad's name and also my grandfather's. But Aussie's love to drop the T, to shorten the name and say "Ocker." Which doesn't have the best connotations in Australia. So, Michael it is.

Dr Haggai gave me medication to treat the food poisoning and together we decided I should stop taking the Lariam tablets and rely instead on mosquito repellent. One of his key instructions was to drink plenty of water. I took that seriously. Knowing that I'd need to drink at least three to four litres a day on the mountain, it became a habit I welcomed.

He was friendly, attentive and professional – and he knew what he was doing.

After lunch, something unexpected happened. I saw a woman walk past the courtyard pergola near the outdoor dining area and I had a hunch I knew who she was. She carries an authority about her and the respect and warmth shown by staff was obvious. I got up, checked with a staff member to confirm and then introduced myself.

It was Mama Zara. I wouldn't realise the full impact of that meeting until later. A hotel upgrade, offering me the complimentary return back a year later and genuine care for her customers.

Mama Zara kindly stopped and chatted for five minutes. I learned that she and her husband had owned Zara Tours for more than thirty years. You could tell from the framed newspaper clippings, the brochures, and the way the staff spoke of her that she was well known, respected and loved. Talking to her, it wasn't hard to see why. Her warmth and humility stood out immediately.

My sister, Michelle, wasn't arriving until later that day, so I used the free afternoon to check out the gear hire area at Springlands Hotel. Zara Tours had a system for hiring quality equipment on-site – snow jacket, poles, sleeping bag, all things I didn't want to travel with. The staff helped me sort through what I needed. It was a helpful, practical step – and a small mental shift, too. For a brief window, my focus wasn't on my troubled stomach. It was on the mountain.

Then I enjoyed a much-needed nap, before Michelle arrived.

It was great to see Michelle again. We've been fortunate to catch up every few years or so, even though we live on different continents. After the usual big hug, we caught up briefly before she settled into her room. It felt good to be taking on another adventure together, the safari the next day and then the mountain.

Five-Day Safari – Calm before the Crisis

It was Friday, the 1st of December 2023.

After breakfast, we met our safari guide, Zamo and began our five-day adventure into the African wilderness. Zamo's warmth and good humour were immediately obvious. From the very first moment, we knew we were in good hands.

I've got a lot more to say about this safari – Zamo, the people, the wildlife, the moments that took our breath away. But as stunning as it all was, that trip is now impossible to separate from what was about to unfold. In fact, it became the backdrop to maybe one of the strangest 40 hours of my life.

Our first stop was Tarangire National Park, where we spent most of the day. The park is well known for its large elephant population, and we weren't disappointed. After our first night near Ngorongoro Crater, we began the journey toward the Serengeti for the second and third-night stay.

It was along the way, that Zamo surprised us with news, that our accommodation had been upgraded. Mama Zara, generously, had decided to move us from the glamping tents we'd booked, into a luxury villa resort owned by Zara Tours. My sister and I had our own rooms, and, for all four nights of the five-day safari, we would be thoroughly spoiled.

There's something about being on safari that stirs your soul. You try to take it all in, to live in the moment, to fully appreciate that this really is one of those once-in-a-lifetime experiences. I remember standing at the Ngorongoro lookout, looking down into the crater below, completely awestruck. It was postcard perfect. A few drifting clouds, but otherwise a crisp, clear view of the crater below with all sorts of game. You really do want to pinch yourself.

From there, we continued into Serengeti National Park, where we would stay in the upgraded lodge for the two nights. As we drove, Zamo gave us insights into the land and the animals. The Serengeti is home to the largest annual migration in the world – over 1.5 million wildebeest, 250,000 zebra and countless gazelles and elands. The place was spellbinding. You feel like you're driving through a National Geographic – seeing so much wild game and receiving info from Zamo.

Funny enough, while Zamo didn't look like the towering Tanzanian Maasai warriors we met along the way, he still had that calm dignity and command of the landscape. Indeed, he sat just high enough to see over the steering wheel and dashboard of the four-wheel drive. The 4WD was kitted out with all our gear, dust on every surface and the pop-top roof we'd already begun to enjoy for game viewing – as he guided us deeper into this iconic wilderness.

After a lovely dinner, we retired to our villas. I was feeling better – confident that the food poisoning and the possible Lariam reaction was behind me and that I'd be fine to start the climb in a few days.

That night felt like a turning point. I went to bed genuinely optimistic, convinced the worst was behind me and looking forward to an early start the next morning.

But just after 'Midnight' everything started…

This was it – the beginning of the 40-hour ordeal I described in the opening chapter. What unfolded over the next two days would test every part of me: physically, mentally and spiritually.

At the time, I didn't fully grasp the seriousness of what was happening.

Serious Medical Condition

Looking back, I now see how close I came to real danger – and how fortunate I was that help was just within reach. Not being able to urinate for over 40 hours wasn't just uncomfortable – it was dangerous. Kidney damage, infection, and even organ failure – all possible.

In the weeks that followed, as I shared my story with friends, family and even strangers, I began doing research. I wanted to understand what had happened to me. I've since learned a lot about men's health – particularly how urinary retention can escalate quickly if untreated. Sharing this story has opened up many conversations I never expected to have and I'm grateful for that.

Here's what I now know: the average 60-year-old male bladder holds up to 500 millilitres. A healthy bladder can stretch to hold more. The scan had shown 740millilitres – already over capacity – but the bag they used to drain mine held over one litre. That means my bladder had already started stretching – and the pressure was rising. I also think about the 30 plus times I tried to go. Even though I was only getting a trickle each time, I'm so relieved my body was releasing something. Had it not, I might have been dealing with even more severe complications.

I'm deeply grateful I got on that plane and that less than eight hours later, I had the very memorable experience of having a catheter inserted. The relief when the catheter was finally inserted was instant. As strange as it sounds, that moment was a blessing. Imagine if I'd still been out in the Serengeti with Zamo, who knows how many hours away from help.

Later, communicating with Dr Haggai after my operation, I learned there are over dozen types of catheters – each designed for different situations. The one I needed, a silicone catheter, just happened to be in Dr Alfred's medical bag when the call came through. That still amazes me.

What you realise afterwards is that, in the thick of it, you're not calculating worst-case scenarios. Your focus is on trying to just cope. The gravity of situation only lands later.

Michelle's Two-Day Safari

When I climbed onto that small plane to get medical help back at Moshi, it meant Michelle would finish the last two days of our planned five-day safari on her own. Of course, there was another question that hung in the air: would she feel like finishing it alone without me?

There was no hesitation. Michelle is a seasoned solo traveller and if there had been, we probably would've asked for two wooden paddles. But there wasn't. Just a quick check-in with Michelle and we both agreed – she was in good hands and would savour the experience.

And we were right.

Michelle couldn't speak more highly of the way Zamo looked after her. His warmth was obvious from the start, but over those two days, his great sense of humour, deep knowledge, and love for the land shone through.

He's one of those people who leaves a lasting impression – not just because of what he does, but how he does it. He speaks several languages and he's studying to become a pilot. I'm personally incredibly grateful for how he handled my emergency – with calm, flexibility and genuine concern. He didn't panic. He adapted. He cared.

Zamo is a true ambassador for Zara Tours and for Tanzania. A heartfelt thank you. We couldn't have been in better hands.

And here's something Michelle and I both agree on – if you're planning to do a safari and a Kilimanjaro climb, **do the safari after**. You'll enjoy it more. Simple as that. It's far more relaxing when you've already conquered the mountain. Before the climb, your mind's racing with prep and pressure. After the summit, you can truly exhale and soak in the magic of the wild.

After everything we'd been through – the safari, the changing plans, that difficult goodbye. Michelle and I made a quiet promise to find something else to take on together. And we did: Fuji San, August 2025, with my sister's son Duncan joining us.

After surviving my 40-hour ordeal, I was catheterized, drained, humbled. After that difficult goodbye with Michelle and Anton and that game-changing lunch with Mario.

I had finally been dropped at the airport to fly home.

The Continuation from Chapter One – Back at the Airport

The Five Flights Home

Well before facing the airport security, I felt the warmth of the urine bag on my right thigh. It was time to drain the bag – not something you want flagged by a body scanner. If I had to drop my pants, I'd rather it was a urine bag – than diamonds and definitely not something worse. Using the small tap attached to the bag, I emptied the contents and tucked everything back into place. A lot more to manage and tuck away – but I got it all back in place and walked through security undetected. No need to drop my pants.

Thankfully, I was flying business class – remember that epic Oman Air deal my travel agent found for me? Absolute legend. Not only did he land that deal, but he also managed to bring all my flights forward so I could get home earlier. That helped – because the journey home for me and my catheter, involved five flights, four stopovers and multiple days of travel:

- Kilimanjaro to Dar es Salaam – approx. 1½ hours, with a midnight hotel stopover.
- Dar se Salaam to Muscat – approx. 6 hours, with a full-day layover and transit airport hotel.
- Muscat to Bangkok – approx. 6 hours, overnight hotel again.
- Bangkok to Sydney – approx. 9½ hours, a long-haul leg.
- And finally, Sydney to Brisbane – approx. 1 hour stretch.

It looks like a lot… because it was. Still, it ended up being much smoother than I expected.

No one asked me to drop my pants. The urine bag strapped to my thigh went undetected, except that one time I forgot to put mobile phone in the tray and I had left it in my right pocket… the same side where the bag was attached.

After my first security check, I learned a few things:

- Always drain the bag right before going through scanners.
- Choose the line with a metal detector rather than a full-body density scanner, if possible.
- Keep the doctor's letter handy, just in case.

At most airports, I sailed through. Most being the operative word.

At Bangkok Airport – 5am, foggy brain – I picked the wrong line. As I stood in the full-body scanner, the screen lit up around my right thigh.

I was pulled aside.

"Empty your pockets," the officer said.

Here it was. This was the moment.

I reached in and – to my surprise – I found my phone. I'd accidentally left it in my pocket instead of putting it in the tray with my other stuff. I handed it over to him, apologised and started putting my shoes back on.

Ever the optimist, I am assumed that was the end of it. Problem detected. Problem solved.

And, sure enough, the officer walked around the scanner and put my mobile in a tray to go through x-ray check. I wasn't asked to go through again. Phew

I picked up my phone and carry-on bag and moved on.

Crisis averted. Just.

It reminded me of that scene in the 2016 movie, *Now You See Me 2*, where the four magicians flick a playing card between them during a security check – smooth, undetected. My setup – a bag and a tube – was a bit bigger than a card… and slightly harder to explain.

By the time I landed in Brisbane, I was both tired and strangely encouraged. Travelling with a catheter and urine bag hadn't been that hard. In fact, like Google had promised, there had been some strange perks. No waiting for seatbelt signs to switch off. No awkward lines. No panic when the 'occupied' light stayed on a bit too long.

I even slept through the night on flights.

Arriving home on a Sunday, the 11th of December 2022 gave me little time to deal with the jetlag before facing what came next. Monday morning brought a new focus: could I get the surgery I needed before Christmas?

It was only two weeks away – I was eager to be rid of the catheter and urine bag as soon as possible.

My wife had been amazing – she'd already spoken to my urologist's office. I was booked for a 'Trial of Void' (TOV) test at Hospital on Monday – a procedure to see if I could urinate naturally once the catheter was removed. We tried but despite tests overseas we could not by-pass this step.

On the 11th of December, my wife drove me in. I completed the paperwork, met the nurse and was explained – that even with my overseas scan and diagnosis, the hospital had its procedures and needed to repeat the same tests.

Fair enough.

The nurse explained that they'd remove the catheter, I'd be monitored, and we'd see if I could urinate on my own. I failed the test within hours. No surprises there.

A new catheter was inserted. This time, I didn't flinch. I knew what was coming.

The nurse called my urologist and gave him the update. I was sent home with a fresh supply of bags and a sinking feeling that surgery before Christmas might not happen.

That evening, I felt frustrated – not just physically, but emotionally too. I still hadn't had the chance to speak directly with my urologist. The next day, while waiting for his call, I found out from his PA that he doesn't perform the robotic prostatectomy. So, I asked his PA for a referral to a doctor who does – and I received one the next day.

While I was waiting for the referral, there was another wait happening… this one halfway around the world, but no less intense.

Michelle & Anton on the Summit

I knew they'd have been woken up before midnight on the 9th of December to begin the climb, aiming to summit at sunrise on the 10th. All I could do was wait and hope. Late that afternoon, Brisbane time, the message finally arrived: Michelle and Anton had made it to the top of Kilimanjaro. I was a thousand kilometres away, but my heart was right there with them – willing them up that mountain.

Michelle later shared how deep she had to dig. Reading her summary, which she posted a few days later, gave me a vivid picture of the willpower she needed to keep going. She was even surprised by how many swear words she knew! It was, without question, one of the toughest things she'd ever done. In that same post she shared just how close she came to giving up – and how much she credits Festo's steady encouragement for getting her to the summit.

WhatsApp Post – 12 Dec 2023, 9:55AM – Author: My sister, Michelle

Kilimanjaro.
Started at midnight at 4600 m, after eating a bowl of porridge. I was unable to sleep before the start. Climbed for 6 hours in a snowstorm and –15 degrees Celsius. We reached the summit at 6:20. At 3am I was ready to quit. I was cold and I was breathing heavily, snot nose, cold hands because my gloves got wet and I felt sorry for myself. I was given sweet tea and dates, the guide's gloves and then pushed through. It was a mental game during several physical challenges. Once we reached the summit, we quickly took a few photos and rushed down. Descent was tricky due to the snow. We got to base camp at 8:50. Slept for an hour and then descended another 7km to 3100m for last night.

Sent from my iPhone

After everything Michelle and I had been through in Serengeti, I didn't want either of them to face the same disappointment I had – having to quit at some point on the mountain. So, when I saw Michelle's message, I felt this wave of relief, pride and – if I'm honest – a touch of wistfulness.

They had done it. Michelle & Anton had made it to the summit.

I was just so glad they both got there moment at *Uhuru Peak*.

Racing the Calendar.

Back in Brisbane, the countdown to Christmas was on – just under two weeks to go and I still didn't have a confirmed surgeon. My impatience got the better of me and I took matters into my hands while waiting for the referral to come through from my urologist office.

I started researching who in Brisbane specialised in the robotic operation Mario had described. That's when I found Dr Boon Kua – based at the Wesley Private Hospital, a five-minute drive on west of CBD. I remembered that he'd done a TURP (Transurethral Resection of the Prostate) for a business colleague and friend a few years earlier.

A quick phone call to a close friend who knew Dr Kua and by the next morning, I had an appointment: Thursday, 13th December at 10:30am.

Thursday couldn't come fast enough. I turned up early to the Wesley Hospital, grateful just to have a confirmed appointment.

Dr Kua welcomed me in and gave me his full attention. I walked him through everything – the safari, the 40-hour ordeal, the catheter, the lunch with Mario. I handed over the scans, blood test results and the letter from Tanzania.

He reviewed everything carefully and confirmed what I already knew: my prostate was *huge*. It needed a significant reduction. Then he said something I didn't expect to hear:

"I'm opening the theatre this Sunday to fit in a few final patients before I go on holiday for Christmas. I can fit you in."

Just like that. A three-hour robotic surgery, as per Mario's suggestion. Only three days away.

I was stunned. And grateful.

Then he did what a good surgeon should do – he talked me through the risks. He explained how the procedure works and what could go wrong. One of the biggest risks was that, if the surrounding muscles or nerves were damaged, I could lose my erectile function.

It wasn't the first time I'd heard this – I'd already been processing it since that lunch with Mario. Still, hearing it again, right before the operation, made it all the more real. When surgery is your only real option, it doesn't make the risks any easier to hear. It was a lot to take in.

But I appreciated the honesty. I'd rather go in fully informed than blind. And the only way through was forward – do the surgery and wait for the outcome.

Heading home, I rang Vicki with the news – I was booked in for surgery in just three days. She was pleased for me. We both knew this was incredible – robotic prostate surgery scheduled just ten days before Christmas.

On Sunday, 17th of December, I caught a taxi to the Wesley for my midday admission. Everything – from the reception staff to the volunteers to the waiting area – was professional, warm and really efficient.

I was scheduled for surgery mid-afternoon but ended up going in later than expected. By the time I came to, it was late evening. I was in a private room on a different floor. Groggy but awake. Safe.

Dr Kua visited me before he clocked off for the day.

He told me he'd been able to remove about 70% of my prostate. The operation had gone well. He didn't believe there was any collateral damage. He confirmed that a few biopsies had been sent off, just to be sure there was no cancer.

I stayed in hospital for two full days and three nights, heading home on Wednesday – four days before Christmas.

It was all about recovery now and I needed help around the house. My wife played nurse and pretty much did everything I couldn't – I wasn't even allowed to drive for a while. I don't recall exactly how long, but it felt forever.

I had another week with the catheter in; to allow healing and to minimise internal pressure. There was still blood in the urine and I had to be extremely careful with any movements or strain in the abdominal area. I slept a lot. Ate more than I should have. Watched heaps of golf. Movies, and more sleep.

Then came Saturday, the 23rd of December – my 61st birthday – now known in our household as *"Free Willy Day"*. Credit goes to my son, Timothy, who coined it after I went back to the hospital to have the catheter removed.

However, there was a catch: I couldn't go home until I proved I could urinate on my own. A proper flow. Nothing forced.

I remembered what Dr Kua had said in that first appointment: "After the operation, you'll be able to *swat flies* on the wall." In other words, I'd be peeing like an 18-year-old again.

I lay there, mobile phone in hand, waiting for the signal from my body.

Eventually, I felt it. I stood up next to the bed, curtain drawn, bottle in hand, ready to catch the first stream.

And then – bam.

It was strong. So strong that I completely missed the opening of the bottle and sprayed the bed sheets.

I'd wet the bed. At a hospital. On my birthday.

The nurses laughed. I laughed. They said I was good to go.

It was official: Free Willy Day was a success!

The next morning, I woke up at home. My first full day without a catheter in over three weeks. Twenty-three days, to be exact.

It was quiet. Peaceful. And I was curious.

I stepped outside into the backyard with one simple goal: to see how strong my stream was. How far I could shoot.

Not in life. Not up a mountain. Just raw urination distance.

This was the true post-op test. And it was glorious.

Chuffed doesn't even begin to describe it. I stood there, aiming like a teenager, watching the arc land halfway across the lawn.

I was grinning. Not just at the distance – though it was impressive – but at what it represented. A body back in flow. A return to something normal. No – better than normal, especially for my age. Something so simple – and honestly, I felt like celebrating. But who with – ha-ha.

And just like that, I was one week into a three-month recovery – a recovery that would give me back my health, my freedom and, eventually, my dream.

It was quieter Christmas than what we had become accustomed to – just Vicki and me at home, with our own family now in different parts of the world. Fortunately, we had the Boxing Day Test on TV – Australia versus Pakistan. Test cricket at its best. Good food, laughter, and space to reflect.

The mountain could wait – but not forever.

In the quiet of those post-Christmas days, I found myself asking different set of what ifs. Not just the climb I'd missed – but about the journey I was unexpectedly on.

The Benefit of Hindsight

As I look back, there are quite a few things I still can't fully explain. There are questions I've asked myself – and questions that have come from family and friends too. To be honest, I've shared this story more times than I can count; at men's breakfast with thirty-odd people and at an evening fundraisers with groups gathered around.

If you were one of those who listened – whether you were genuinely interested or just too polite to escape my enthusiasm – thank you. It's had a profound impact on me, realising how many people have taken a genuine interest in this journey and what happened along the way.

Here are just a few of the questions that have come up:

- What if had stuck with the original plan to do the safari after the climb?
- What if we hadn't been upgraded to that lodge where I ended up meeting Dr Godwin – all because I'd met Mama Zara three days earlier?
- Why didn't I consider the possibility that my prostate was the problem? It took Dr Godwin to mention it after testing for a UTI. In hindsight, I think I was too focused on recovering from food poisoning and second-guessing the effects of the malaria tablets to imagine a third issue was at play.
- Why didn't we discuss the option of a helicopter evacuation – especially after Dr Godwin told us about the Danish guy who'd needed one earlier that year for the same issue?
- Why not have a catheter on hand in the middle of Serengeti for emergencies? All interesting ideas – after the fact. Mine was not the only case.
- Why didn't we call to check when was the next flight out of the Serengeti to Arusha was?
- What if we hadn't pulled up at the airport when we did?
- What if I'd insisted on stopping for a leak earlier and not waited for the building Zamo pointed out when I first asked if we could stop?
- What would have happened if I'd told the airport staff, I needed urgent medical help? Would they have put me on a direct flight to Arusha instead of routing through two more stops?

- And how do you explain the whole experience – paying US$250 cash, getting a wooden paddle instead of a boarding pass, no health declaration, no forms? I was so fortunate. Yes, it was unconventional. And strangely… I loved it. It felt like a moment from another time – a throwback to when travel was simpler, less bureaucratic. A refreshing contrast to the compliance-heavy world we navigate back home.
- Was it wrong that I didn't inform the airline staff or pilots about my medical situation?
- Why didn't I think to take on board with me an empty bottle in case I needed to go mid-flight? It such a small thing, but something I hadn't adjusted to doing differently.
- What if Dr Alfred hadn't had the silicone catheter in his medical bag?

So many 'what ifs?'.

For now, let's just say I was very fortunate to get out of the Serengeti when I did.

At the time, I didn't grasp how close I was to the line. I'm grateful that I made that flight – and that later that day, I received the treatment I urgently needed – just in time.

Complimentary Consultation – Mario (Urologist)?

Then came my lunch with Mario, the urologist. Wow.

I learned more during that one meal than I had in five years of regular check-ups. He talked me through the four different types of prostate operations and how one in three men over the age of 50 will end up needing one. It was because of that unexpected lunch that I even knew about and asked for the robotic procedure to reduce the size of my prostate, rather than the more common option that simply improves flow through the urethra (the rebore approach).

Had I gone with the 'rebore' approach, I likely would've needed another one in eight to ten years. That's because my prostate was already increasing in size. The robotic procedure addressed the root issue, not just the symptom.

That lunch with Mario led to the exact operation I needed. Thank you, Mario.

And perfectly timed, just before Christmas and only twelve days after the catheter was first inserted. Did I mention how nerve-racking that first-time experience was?

In Brisbane, my urologist had been monitoring my condition for five years. He's a strong believer in not operating too early, preferring to wait until the benefits clearly outweigh the risks. And rightly so. At the time, I didn't fully appreciate that approach. When you feel healthy and strong, it's hard to imagine that anything serious might go wrong as result of any procedure – such as losing erectile function.

At my most recent check-up, just six months before Tanzania, he still felt surgery could wait. To deal with the issue of waking multiple times each night, he recommended a medication I could try, designed to relax the prostate and ease the pressure on the bladder.

Looking back, I'm grateful for his cautious, considered approach.

My Delayed Summit – I Will Be Back

I can see that even in the midst of the setback, even while bringing my flights forward and facing surgery, I never lost the desire to climb Kilimanjaro. In fact, I still can't believe it crossed my mind for a brief moment to climb with a catheter and a urine bag strapped to my underpants… but I did. That was the very evening Michelle and Anton were sitting down for their Kili briefing with Festo. I had actually wondered if I could just get on the bus with them the next morning.

I'd invested so much over the previous twelve months. The research. The more than one hundred hours hiking the southeast corner of Queensland. The medical check-ups. The gear. The mindset work. The mindset work. It all meant something.

I still needed to see it through.

Even as I boarded that flight out of Kilimanjaro, I knew what I'd told Mama Zara and Erasto wasn't just a nice goodbye – it was a promise. I *was* going to come back. And hopefully, I wouldn't be coming alone.

This was just a pause – not the end. The mountain would wait.

Somewhere along the way, the summit had become secondary to the journey. The growth. The transformation. I remember saying to myself, "Michael, time to enjoy the journey."

After my operation, I remember talking with Michelle and Anton about their success. It's hard to put into words the difference between hearing about someone's summit on YouTube and hearing it from someone you know – someone you love. When I spoke to them afterward, I could feel it. The high. The pride. The transformation. Something had changed in them.

It reminded me of that iconic line from *When Harry Met Sally* – *"I'll have what she's having."*

Somehow, I knew I still would.

I was going back to have my high. (Pun intended.)

"A man too busy to take care of his health is like a mechanic too busy to take care of his tools."

– Proverb

CHAPTER SIX

RECOVERY, REFLECTION
AND RENEWAL

Operation successful, how fortunate was I? To have undergone a
robotic prostatectomy, a minimally invasive procedure, where a
surgeon removes part or all of the prostate gland using advanced tech-
nology with remarkable precision. In my case, about seventy percent
of the centre of the gland was removed. As part of the downsize, a few
biopsies were taken to check for cancer – just to be safe.

The robot-assisted surgery allowed the specialist to operate with
enhanced control and visibility, which in turn reduced recovery time
and the risk of complications. In retrospect, I can appreciate how
incredibly fortunate I was to have access to that level of medical care. It
gave me the best possible outcome.

And to think it all hinged on that serendipitous lunch with Mario.
Our conversation led me to Google, on 12th December with the question: "Who in Brisbane does robotic prostate surgery?"

Just two days later, after a friend made that call for me I was sitting in Dr Kua's office. Three days after that, I was wheeled into theatre for a three-hour operation – on Sunday, the 17th of December. All before Christmas.

Writing and sharing this again reminds me just how incredible the whole sequence was. I remain in awe of how well and how fast I was looked after.

Time for Recovery

With the catheter removed six days after my operation – on my 61st birthday, no less – it was time to focus on recovery.

When I was being discharged three days after surgery, Dr Kua let me know he'd arranged for a hospital day visit to remove the catheter. I expected it would be a quick in-and-out, but I ended up there for four or five hours. I wasn't allowed to leave until I could prove I was able to urinate. So, the plan was simple; drink water, fill up the bladder, wait for the urge and then go.

Easier said than done. I wasn't complaining – far from it. I actually saw the humour in it. Less than two weeks earlier, when I desperately needed to go, I couldn't. And now, I couldn't go… because my bladder was empty!

Eventually, after a lot of water and patience, I was cleared. I was discharged, having only had one minor mishap – the wet bed. As grateful as I am for the doctors, nurses and the exceptional care at the Wesley Hospital, I left with an inner goal: to see how many years I could go without needing to be back.

It had already been a big year of operations, three including the two I had earlier in preparation for Kilimanjaro. My body had been through enough.

Dr Kua advised me to expect a three-month recovery (around 12 to 15 weeks), and handed me a clear list of what I *wasn't* allowed to do until my post-op appointment: no sit-ups; no long walks; no hiking Mount Coot-tha; no gym workouts; no swimming; no cycling; no golf; no squash.

In other words, none of the things I enjoy doing. Really, a small price to pay.

That said, if you're going to be forced into downtime, Christmas and New Year isn't a bad stretch of time to do very little. And for me, it ended up being a surprisingly lovely time. The days passed quickly – Christmas, video calls with extended family, New Year's celebrations, lots of reading, a bit of Netflix, watching test cricket, tennis, and a few brunches.

I'm incredibly grateful to my wife for all the help and running around she did. I know she would've preferred us to be doing some of the other things we normally enjoy at that time of year. She ended up not having the holiday break away from home that she was hoping for. But it was a different kind of season for us... and that was okay. We adjusted – I was home safe.

The Doctor's Call – Post Operation

About ten days after the operation, in that peaceful pocket between Christmas and New Year, I received an unexpected call from Dr Kua. I knew he was on holidays, which made it all the more impressive. He rang to check in on how I was doing – and to prepare me for something.

He asked whether there was still any blood in my urine. I told him it was noticeably less than before. He then gently warned me that I might soon see *more* blood again. As part of the body's healing process, the internal scarring within the prostate can loosen and cause temporary bleeding.

Indeed, if he had not made that call, I'm almost certain I would've asked my wife to drive me straight to hospital. Sure enough, the bleeding did increase over the following days and had I not been reassured ahead of time, I would've become concerned. Thankfully, it all settled again within ten days or so.

He also brought up what I now call *The Erection Question* – again. He made it very clear that, while most physical activities were off the table, sex wasn't on the banned list.

I admit that this surprised me – especially considering what *was* on the banned list. No swimming. No golf. No walking Mount Coot-tha. But yes, apparently that particular form of exercise got a green light.

I figured the question had something to do with checking whether the nerves and muscles responsible for erectile function had been preserved.

What's amazed me since then is just how often I've been asked about it. And the different ways that people have found to ask! Blokes. Mates. Even acquaintances. There's a certain curiosity.

And of course, there's the classic: "So, Michael… can you still… *[cheeky whistle]*?"

No words needed – just the sound. And we all know exactly what they mean.

My answer? Yes. I can.

The advantage of the robotic prostatectomy is that the surgeon can carefully remove the problematic tissue while avoiding damage to the erectile nerves and muscles. This was discussed before the operation and assessed afterwards, to ensure everything was still working as it should.

Considering I really had no choice but to have the operation. So, I am incredibly grateful to the doctor that there was no unnecessary damage.

Bladder Control

There was a period – maybe four to six weeks – when I was retraining my bladder muscles. The goal was to get them holding the amount of fluid they were once capable of. It was a weird sort of training regime and definitely more mental than physical.

Things were manageable at home but, when I was out and about, it became a different story. I became a toilet scout – always wanting to know where the nearest toilets were before saying yes to a brunch, shopping, or any outing that involved more than one stop.

There was one outing I remember vividly, mostly because it didn't go so well. My bladder muscles just didn't hold on long enough. Before I could unzip, I'd had an accident. That meant a quick change of plans, a drive home and a change of clothes. Humbling, to say the least.

But with persistence – and a real effort to become aware of how those muscles felt and functioned – I gradually gained control again. I could feel the small wins along the way; fewer urges, longer gaps between trips to the toilet and eventually, more nights when I slept through without needing to get up.

Now? I can wait until morning. And for the record – I don't need to visit the backyard. We don't have a lemon tree.

Biopsy – Benign or Positive

In the back of my mind and my wife's too, there was an unspoken question hanging over us like the proverbial elephant in the room.

Consciously, we weren't dwelling on it. But the absence of a call from Dr Kua, or his office, kept tugging at something in the background: what were the biopsy results?

The longer we waited, the more we leaned into the idea that *no news is good news*. We both figured that if the results had come back positive, we'd have heard earlier. Still, not knowing does something to you. It's a silent weight you carry, whether you talk about it or not.

It wasn't until my post-op appointment on the 13th of February 2024 that we finally found out. The biopsy was negative – no cancer. Just a benign enlargement, exactly as we'd hoped. I remember the moment Dr Kua told me. It was a huge relief.

In retrospect, there was a part of me that didn't really want to know the result before Christmas. I just wanted to enjoy the season. The cricket. The New Year. The recovery. I wanted space to relax and not have to prepare for another surgery.

A positive result would have meant more surgery, more decisions, more uncertainty. After everything I'd already been through, the thought of that was too much.

As soon as I got the all-clear, I let the family know. It felt like the final piece of that chapter had dropped into place. I was able to deeply exhale after six weeks of not knowing.

Then, just as I thought the loose ends were tied up, another unexpected thread appeared.

Travel Insurance

Here's something I didn't expect to be part of the recovery story: travel insurance.

Before the trip, I'd made sure to pay for my flights using my credit card, which triggered the complimentary coverage offered through bank.

After the operation, I submitted a claim, thinking it would be fairly straightforward – especially after my phone conversations in December. But then came a surprise.

They contacted me to say the claim might be denied, because I hadn't disclosed the fact that I'd been monitored for a benign enlarged prostate by my urologist over the previous five years. *Ag nee (oh no),* I thought to myself that I know better. I should've brought it to the insurer's attention.

To the insurance companies credit, they didn't reject it outright. They made further enquiries, reviewed the records from my regular check-ups and satisfied themselves that I had done everything responsibly – and hadn't taken any unnecessary risks by going on the trip. In the end, they paid the claim in full.

I was impressed. That kind of fair handling matters – and it taught me something to avoid the hiccup altogether: declare everything. Even if it seems minor or 'benign', disclose it.

Exercise & Work

After my post-op appointment, I was cleared to start easing back into physical activity – but gently. I began with short walks of under an hour and some light swimming during weeks seven to ten. No hiking, no gym, no squash, no cycling and definitely no sit-ups. Even in the pool, I could feel the pull on my abdominal muscles, so I kept to a slow, lazy breaststroke and stayed low in the water.

By early February, around six weeks after the operation, I started popping back into the office for the occasional morning. That transition was something in itself. I found myself sharing the story of what had happened – my unexpected medical adventure in the Serengeti – and, to my surprise, people genuinely wanted to hear it.

Friends, family, colleagues, even clients. Everyone seemed curious and not just for the dramatic details. I was grateful for the way they listened. And while I certainly appreciated the seriousness of what I'd been through, I also found the funny side. There were just so many strange, serendipitous events. Telling the story became part of my own processing.

So, to all of you who listened – thank you.

Sharing My Story

What surprised me most in those early months was how sharing my story sparked so many unexpected conversations – and connections. It became more than just retelling the Serengeti saga. It opened doors to deeper discussions and I'm incredibly grateful for that.

I found myself talking less about the dramatic medical moment and more about everything that surrounded it. Conversations naturally drifted toward men's health, resilience and the idea of living a more balanced life.

People started opening up – more than I ever expected. Some shared their own health scares. Others spoke about friends or family members facing similar challenges. One conversation really stuck with me. A man approached me after a small office team workshop and told me, softly, that he'd recently been diagnosed with prostate cancer. He was booked in for the same operation I'd had – just a few weeks away.

These weren't just medical conversations. They often segued into talk about *bucket lists* – adventures people still wanted to chase. Some ideas were so intriguing I found myself Googling them afterward, even adding a few to my own list.

But what truly caught me off guard was how many people, after hearing my story, asked the same question, "Michael… are you going back?"

The moment I responded 'yes' that I was, something shifted. I wasn't telling a story anymore – I was answering questions about Kilimanjaro. People were starting to wonder if it was something they could do too. Some even talked about joining me.

That's when (and why) I started calling it the 'Ripple Effect'.

What I started to notice is, after sharing my story, people would show interest in joining me on the climb and they would also think of somebody that might be interested too.

What stood out again and again were two things that seemed to matter most to people:

1. The pull toward a life that's living – not just existing.
2. The importance of men's health.

It became clear this story wasn't just mine – it echoed deeply with things others were feeling too. A desire to live more fully. To face fears. To prioritise what really matters.

The Importance of Men's Health

Of course, wanting to live fully is one thing – *being able to* is another.

Men's health is often a whispered topic – something we joke about, dodge, or leave until it's too late. But the truth is, regular check-ups matter. Prostate health, cholesterol, blood pressure, heart function, mental well-being – these aren't just 'nice to know' things. They're essential.

I've come to realise that a yearly visit to the doctor isn't just a tick-the-box exercise. It's peace of mind. It's about catching things before they catch you – ideally *before* you're halfway across the world in the middle of Serengeti, miles from a hospital.

I do think there's a mindset shift happening in society. Men are slowly learning to talk about their health – not just with doctors, but with each other and with their families. I'm rather fortunate to be part of two different groups of mates where this kind of talk is not only okay, but encouraged.

The first is the Elite Athletes (EAs) – our annual challenge crew, which I've already mentioned built around fitness, sweat and adventure. But the second group? The long-standing card buddies: "The Musketeers."

We play the card game 500 about eight times a year, mostly on Friday nights and once a year we up the ante with a long weekend away – a full three-day card marathon. It's not about the physical challenge – it's about the banter, the meat-heavy meals like *boerewors* (or farmer's sausage), the laughter, the singing, the recycled jokes, always the good South African liqueur – *Amarula* – and yes, the fierce desire to win.

The scribe keeps the official book – proof of past wins and losses. Who knows, maybe one day we'll even look at the stats.

There's always a full house, not just in the card sense. We literally can't play unless all four of us can make it. That's the beauty of 500; it only works with four. If someone can't make it, the night's off. No subs. No reshuffles. Just a non-intrusive message in our WhatsApp group and we start looking for the next available date the four of us can make – *one for all, all for one.*

Two very different groups. But a common thread for me and both groups? Is we talk. We check in. And somewhere between the climbing and the card games, most of us have made our annual health check-ups a non-negotiable part of life.

What I have come to realise is that being willing to share my story has made it easier for other men to share theirs. That same man I mentioned earlier, the one who was booked in for prostate surgery, later told me something that's stayed with me. He'd known about the prostate cancer for a few months, had put in for leave at work, but hadn't told anyone. I was the first person outside his family he'd opened up to.

There was something sacred about that moment – realising I was the first person he'd told. It reminded me how many men carry things secretly, waiting for someone to give them permission to speak.

We caught up for coffee not long after and we talked openly – not just about the surgery, but the anxiety, the questions, the what-ifs. After the operation, when all the tests came back, he rang to share the news: he had received the 'all clear'.

"What we don't need in the midst of struggle is shame for being human." - Brene Brown

There's something powerful about hearing someone else's story. It helps you face your own. I've had men reach out, ask questions, share their experiences – and even book doctor's appointments they'd been putting off for years.

If my story helps even one person act, then it's already worth it.

The Adventurous, Balanced Life

Sharing my experience opened up another unexpected line of conversation – the call to more challenges and adventures, finding out what others have thought about doing.

I always knew there was something powerful about planning my return to climb Kilimanjaro. But I didn't realise how many others were carrying that same itch for challenge. Once I started telling my story, people lit up. Friends. Family. Even strangers.

My local bank manager is one of them. Her eyes lit up when we got talking. Turns out she'd had three decades of adventures under her belt. Hearing her stories reminded me that people around us are often full of ambition we know nothing about. You just need the right conversation to bring it out and get to know that side of them.

People started asking questions:

Why Kilimanjaro?
When are you going?
How are you preparing?
Who's going with you?
Do you think I could do it tooz0?

I started uncovering this shared adventurous spirit. Some said they'd love to climb it one day. Others knew people who had tried but didn't make it – altitude sickness often being the culprit. That got me thinking hard about my own mental preparation.

One of those conversations was with a good friend, James, who I'd originally meet through professional circles. In his early 40s, he told me his father had summited years ago and, ever since, it's been quietly sitting on his radar too. Hearing James' desire – and so many other stories like it – made me realise just how many people are carrying around a dream, waiting for the right moment.

Which leads to the deeper question: how do you fit it in? Or better: how do you make it happen? That's the real task, isn't it?

Plenty of people talk about chasing adventure, but they also admit they're struggling to make space for it. I get it. Life is full – work, family, commitments. But if you truly want to go for something, you find a way. Once you lock in a challenge, everything else begins to adjust around it. That's the key – deciding on something.

If I can encourage you – find one adventure, lock it in and then decide how often you want to lock one in. It doesn't have to be Kilimanjaro. But set your sights on something. Because when you do, it helps recalibrate life's balance and gives you something to work toward that's bigger than the inbox or the to-do list.

What makes it even more meaningful is doing it with others – people who want to take that journey with you. That's when it becomes more than a goal. That's when it becomes a memory.

This was starting to look very promising.

Back to Tanzania – But Not Alone This Time

That's the part that truly surprised me – sharing my story didn't just spark conversation. It inspired action.

Friends who'd heard what happened weren't just asking about Kilimanjaro out of curiosity. They were seriously considering it. They wanted to be part of something. Suddenly, the climb wasn't just mine anymore. It was becoming something bigger – a growing group of adventurers.

If you'd told me back then that in the end, I'd be facilitating a group of ten to summit the mountain, I would've laughed and said, "I'd love that... but I have no idea where those people would come from."

But they came. And the ripple effect was real. What began as a personal goal had become a collective momentum – something that felt, in a strange way, like it was meant to happen.

It gave me a whole new appreciation for that old saying: It's about the journey, not just the destination.

But I'd add something to that: It's also about who you take the journey with.

So, when you plan your next adventure, maybe the real question isn't just, "What do I want to do?" Maybe it's, "Who do I want to do it with?"

And that's how **The Ripple Effect** began.

🔋 Men's Annual Health Check-ups by Decade

Because staying on the mountain starts with staying on top of your health.

◈ In Your 30s
- Blood Pressure Check: Every 1-2 years
- Cholesterol and Lipids: Baseline check, then every 5 years
- Skin Check: Especially for Aussies – full-body skin exam every 1-2 years
- Testicular Exam: Regular self-checks; discussion with GP
- Mental Health: Do not wait for burnout – check in annually
- Weight and Waist Circumference: Body composition starts to shift

◈ In Your 40s
- Prostate Health: Begin discussions with GP, especially with family history
- Diabetes Screening: Fasting blood sugar or HbA1c every 3-5 years
- Eye Exam: Every 2-4 years, watch for early signs of glaucoma
- Heart Health: Include ECG and family history assessment
- Bowel Health: Baseline screening may start depending on risk

◈ In Your 50s
- Prostate Specific Antigen (PSA) Test: Annually, or as advised
- Bowel Cancer Screening: Begin biennial FOBT (Faecal Occult Blood Test)
- Bone Density (DEXA): Especially if family history or risk factors
- Hearing Test: Every 2-3 years
- Vaccinations: Shingles, flu and pneumococcal as recommended

◈ In Your 60s and Beyond
- Cognitive Screening: Memory, mood and brain health
- Vision and Hearing: Yearly exams recommended
- Heart and Circulatory Health: Consider coronary calcium scan or stress testing
- Mobility and Falls Risk: Balance, strength and gait checks
- Skin, Prostate and Bowel: Keep up regular checks
- Medication Review: Annual review for interactions and side effects

✅ *Tip: Bring a written list of questions to your check-up. Make the most of those 15 minutes – your future self will thank you.*

Source - ChatGPT Prompts.

COMMON PROSTATE SURGERIES

1. Transurethral Resection of the Prostate (TURP)
- Procedure: A surgical procedure where a surgeon removes a portion of the prostate tissue that is blocking urine flow.
- Indication: Benign prostatic hyperplasia (BPH), a non-cancerous enlargement of the prostate.
- Goal: To relieve urinary symptoms such as weak stream, frequent urination and urgency.

2. Open Prostatectomy
- Procedure: A surgical procedure where a surgeon removes the entire prostate gland or a portion of it through an incision in the abdomen.
- Indication: BPH or prostate cancer.
- Goal: To remove the prostate tissue that is causing urinary symptoms, or to remove cancerous tissue.

3. Laparoscopic Radical Prostatectomy (LRP)
- Procedure: A minimally invasive surgical procedure where a surgeon removes the prostate gland using a laparoscope and specialized instruments.
- Indication: Prostate cancer.
- Goal: To remove the cancerous prostate gland while preserving surrounding nerves and tissues.

4. Holmium Laser Enucleation of the Prostate (HoLEP)
- Procedure: A minimally invasive surgical procedure where a surgeon uses a holmium laser to remove prostate tissue that is blocking urine flow.
- Indication: BPH.
- Goal: To relieve urinary symptoms by removing prostate tissue while preserving surrounding tissues.

5. Robotic-Assisted Laparoscopic Radical Prostatectomy (RALRP)
- Procedure: A minimally invasive surgical procedure where a surgeon uses a robotic system (e.g., da Vinci Surgical System) to remove the prostate gland.
- Indication: Prostate cancer.
- Goal: To remove the cancerous prostate gland while preserving surrounding nerves and tissues.

BENEFITS OF ROBOTIC PROCEDURE:
- Improved precision: Enhanced visualisation and precise dissection.
- Less blood loss: Reduced risk of bleeding and transfusions.
- Faster recovery: Less post-operative pain and quicker return to normal activities.
- Better outcomes: Potential for improved cancer control and reduced side effects.

TYPICAL DURATION:
- 2-4 hours: Robotic procedure itself
- 4-6 hours: Including prep, anaesthesia and recovery

STEPS and APPROXIMATE TIMES:
1. Preparation and anaesthesia: 30 min to 1 hr.
2. Robotic prostatectomy: 2-4 hrs.
3. Lymph node dissection (if needed): 30 min to 1 hr.
4. Closure and recovery: 1-2 hrs.

Source - ChatGPT Prompts.

"I learned that courage was not the absence of fear, but the triumph over it."

– Nelson Mandela

CHAPTER SEVEN

✦

THE RIPPLE EFFECT: FORMING THE GROUP

Unbelievable. Incredible. Fantastic. That's still how I feel when I think about how this amazing group of ten ended up travelling to Tanzania in January 2025 to tackle *The Roof of Africa*. I remain both surprised and incredibly grateful for how it all unfolded.

I remembered telling Erasto, the tour manager at Zara Tours, that I'd try to bring a few friends. But because of the experience trying to get people to join us the first time I wasn't making any promises. Who really takes time off, flies to Africa and climbs a 6,000-metre mountain just because you suggest it? One or two would've been a great result.

But then, something unexpected happened.

I bumped into an old friend Deb on the 3rd of February 2024. We hadn't caught up in years. Back when our children were in primary school, Deb and her husband Ken were neighbours. Our families had shared plenty of times together. So naturally, we grabbed a coffee to reconnect.

Before long, Kilimanjaro came up.

"Michael, are you going back?" she asked.

"Yes," I replied. "And I'm looking for people to join me."

Her response came without hesitation, "I'd love to join you."

It caught me off guard – in a good way. Deb's always had quite an adventurous streak. She loves the outdoors and has a real passion for "thru-walking" – those multi-day, overnight walks "through" a national park. I knew that Deb and her husband had done loads of outrigger paddling and canoeing throughout the Pacific over the years, but this was something different. A mountain. A big one. And she was in.

What struck me most was how easily things started to fall into place. Just a year earlier, my sister, brother-in-law and I had tried to grow the group to half a dozen with no success. Not even one mere person. But now? One conversation led to another. I don't fully understand why it worked this time. Maybe it was the story. Maybe it was timing.

Maybe it was just the right mix of people looking for something more.

Whatever it was, the ripple effect had begun.

The Power of the Info Night

Deb and I planned the first information night. I remembered how impactful the session in Amsterdam had been for my sister and her decision to say yes to Kilimanjaro. That stuck with me. I wanted this night to be helpful, but I was very aware of one key difference; unlike the presenter in Amsterdam, I hadn't summited the mountain yet.

I was still dealing with unanswered questions.

Would I make it this time? What's it really like up there? What's the hardest day? How do people handle altitude? What gear makes the difference on summit night?

We set the date: Wednesday, the 7th of April 2024. The venue? My office boardroom – affectionately called the Green Room because of the green wall paint. That was about two months after my coffee with Deb. I mention that because the ripple effect wasn't instant; it was gradual.

There were many conversations taking place behind the scenes between Deb and her cousin, her friends and others. And rightly so. Saying yes to an adventure like Kilimanjaro is no small decision. It takes time. You're committing to eight days on a mountain, on another continent, at nearly 6,000 metres. That's not something people say yes to overnight.

For the first information night, the guest list was modest: Deb; her cousin Belinda; and her friends Amanda – 'Moo' (as she prefers to be called), and Libby (who joined via a video call from Melbourne). There was also one no-show. Still, we had a strong little group.

I emailed Erasto at Zara Tours in advance to let him know the evening was happening and sent him a few questions. Thankfully, I had all the material from my original planned trip. I dug out the 100-day training plan, route info, cost breakdowns, gear lists and helpful YouTube clips. I bundled everything into a booklet, bound and printed. It turned out to be well received and appreciated.

To be fully transparent, I knew Deb was putting her trust in me. She was introducing her network to something big – and to me. I didn't want to blow the opportunity of having a great group to do the climb with by winging it. So, I put together a run sheet – not too formal, more like a helpful flow – and made sure I covered all the things that had helped me come to a decision the first time.

In classic Deb fashion, she turned up with homemade baking. Libby being on the video call unfortunately missed out, but the rest of us enjoyed it while we talked. It didn't take long for me to realise I was sitting with a very capable group of women – women who were no strangers to adventure. This challenge didn't scare them. Sure, it was big, but for them it was just another mountain – literally and figuratively.

That first night was more than catch-up; it was the spark. As we sat around sharing stories, asking questions and tossing around possibilities, I saw the effectiveness of bringing people together for an information night – a contemplative, no-pressure evening.

Why Information Nights Work

The dynamics of the decision-making process individuals go through, especially when it comes to something as big as climbing Kilimanjaro, shouldn't be underestimated. And after witnessing it firsthand, I've become a big believer in the power of the information night. Not as a sales tool, but as a space to genuinely support people through their own process.

Let me explain what I noticed.

Every person comes at this kind of decision differently. For some, it's about cost. For others, it's health or time away from family. Some need to understand every detail before they commit. Others just want to know they're not doing it alone. That's why a group information night is so powerful – it meets people where they are.

Here's why they work so well:

- **Shared Energy and Enthusiasm:** When a group of like-minded people comes together in the same room to talk about a big idea, there's a natural buzz. You can feel it. One person's excitement feeds the next. That kind of energy is contagious – it transforms curiosity into possibility.

- **Clarity and Confidence:** Everyone wants to know what they're getting into. An info night lays it all out – what the trip looks like, how much it costs, what training is involved and what gear you'll need. Clarity builds confidence and confidence leads to commitment.

- **Group Accountability:** Once someone says "I'm keen" in front of others, it becomes real. There's something powerful about voicing intent aloud, especially in a room full of potential teammates. It's no longer just an idea; it's a decision taking shape.

- **Addressing Fears and Concerns:** Everyone has doubts. Will I get altitude sickness? Will I be fit enough? Can I handle the cold? In a group setting, those questions get asked and answered. Shared stories and honest responses (first and second hand) take the edge off the fear and replace it with practical hope.

- **Momentum Through Community:** Before the night is even over, people start making plans – who they'll train with, where to buy gear, when to hike. You don't have to push anyone. The momentum builds naturally because people are doing it together.

- **Visualising the Journey:** When you walk through maps, routes, past experiences and stories, it helps people *see* themselves on the mountain. You watch it change in their mind, from a distant dream to a reachable summit.

When you look at the group dynamics, it's clear that information nights do something special — they give people space to process things in their own way. And that process, I've come to realise, is more layered and personal than most of us think.

Decision Making Process

Here are the six main factors I observed that people wrestle with before saying yes to something like Kilimanjaro. It's almost worthy of a flowchart.

- **Cost and Affordability:** Between flights, visas, gear, vaccinations, insurance, and the climb itself, there's no denying it's a significant investment.
- **Physical and Health Preparedness:** Some need medical clearance; others have to overcome previous injuries or build confidence in their fitness. Everyone asks, "Can I physically do this?"
- **Time Commitment:** Eight days on the mountain plus travel time, and potential altitude time before. This is a big chunk out of a busy life. Fitting in training with work schedules, school terms, and family responsibilities all come into play.
- **Group Fit:** People need to feel like they belong with the group. It's not just about personalities, it's about shared purpose, energy, and attitude.
- **Family and Social Support:** For many, it's not just their decision. They want their partner, kids, or friends, to support the idea – or at least not worry too much. The adventure does not just need a passport; it needs your family's okay.
- **Perceived Risk and Safety:** Altitude, weather, medical care and 'what if' scenarios. These fears are real, and some people need time to work through them.

That insight was obvious throughout our process. A well-run information night touches each of these areas. And more importantly, it helps people get over the unknown and face fears and it does so without pressure. I made a conscious effort not to push. My role was to encourage, inform and support, not to persuade. Looking back, I'm still amazed that ten people said yes.

In total, sixteen were seriously considering it. Of the six who didn't come, most had two or more of those decision factors holding them back. A couple had just one. Family support stood out as a big one. If we'd been planning an Everest summit, I suspect all sixteen would've needed that green light. Interestingly, four of the six never made it to an information night. Two joined a training hike and you could tell they were right on the edge of saying yes. I'm convinced that if the other two had come along to a session, we might've added one or two more to the team.

That's a takeaway I'll carry forward; open the invite to partners and loved ones. When people see the visuals and feel the energy in the room, their fears soften. Decisions feel safer. Supported.

So yes, I'm a huge fan of information nights, they help with the decision process. They don't just inform – they empower. For the record, I'm still hoping to take those six on a future trip. They'll get another crack at the decision process and who knows, maybe you, the reader, will too. The ripple effect is still going...

WhatsApp Group Momentum

After that first session, Deb and I began spreading the word. She set up our WhatsApp group – *Kilimanjaro Community*. Later, it expanded into subgroups: Training; Gear; Travel. It helped a lot. Searching through chat history became easier and people could find what they needed without scrolling endlessly.

Choosing the Climb Dates

One of the first group decisions we needed to make was when to go. I told Deb I hadn't locked in dates and wanted it to be a collective choice. After some back-and-forth, we narrowed it down to three options: pre-Christmas, late January (to align with the Australia Day long weekend), or mid-February.

Late January won. It gave us time to train over the holidays and the long weekend worked for most. I emailed Erasto and locked in the Lemosho Route – an eight-day climb starting Friday the 24th of January 2025, aiming to summit on the 30th.

We made a special request that we would like to go ahead subject to Festo's availability to be our guide. That request had been shaped by a conversation I had with Michelle after her climb. The one where she told me to the 8-day Lemosho Route. Her experience with Festo as her guide had cemented it for me. I'd asked her: "What would you do differently next time?"

Her response was immediate: "Do the 8-day, not the 7-day climb. On the 7-day climb, the second day is brutal. On the 8-day, it's split into two manageable parts."

Advice taken.

At that stage, I told Erasto to expect maybe six or eight people. Ha! Even then, I hadn't imagined we'd hit ten.

Continuing to Grow the Group

The opportunity to share my Serengeti story continued to open doors. But there was a noticeable shift. When people asked, "Michael, are you going back?" I wasn't just saying yes for myself anymore – I was saying, "Yes and at this stage, there are four women on board: Deb, Moo, Belinda, and Libby."

I would end up sharing some of the challenges that I had learned that four of them had taken on individually, with others, with one another over the years. It was inspiring. For them, it wasn't a once-off idea; adventure seemed like a way of life – something they actively sought out. A few months after I was introduced to Deb's group of friends, one of them let the WhatsApp group know about a documentary doing the rounds: *Gutsy Girls*. Their interest didn't surprise me one bit. I was grateful for the company I was now keeping.

Around the same time, I reached out to my Elite Athlete mates to see if any of them might be up for the climb. Three had to rule it out early for various reasons – like the one we covered earlier. One gave it some serious thought – he was keen to do it as a father–son experience with his boy, who had not long finishing high school. In the end, the timing just didn't line up.

I tried rescheduling the next information night a few times to accommodate the guys I'd been talking to. Eventually, I decided to go ahead with whoever could make it and planned to catch up for coffee with the others individually.

Second Information Night – Tuesday, 25th June 2024

This time, it was a smaller group, four guys: Brent, Dan, Dave, me.

As a result of that evening, Dan (Belinda's husband) and Dave committed to the trip over the following month. I sent another update to Erasto – our number was growing.

Around that same time, just before the end of June, I decided it was time to reach out to someone in past... the first person I immediately thought of when Erasto first asked me to try and bring people back with. Back in my room at Springlands Hotel, it was our shared dream to climb Kilimanjaro that surfaced – unfinished, unspoken. I wasn't ready then, but it was now time to try.

So, I did. Quietly. I passed a message along through our wider circle – not directly, but gently. I didn't want to intrude or stir anything unwelcome. The message made it, I received a kind, warm response. But a no none the less. Still, I'm glad I honoured the impulse. It felt like something that needed to be done. to acknowledge a friendship that had once meant a great deal and a shared dream that never quite found its moment.

The group-building process wasn't always formal. Sometimes it was just a casual chat over breakfast, a sushi lunch, or a story shared during a business networking event.

One of the more fruitful catchups happened late July, when Dave and I met up. Over some breakfast and a good coffee, we talked through who else might be a good fit for the team. Andy's name came up.

We realised we both knew Andy; and Dave knew Kilimanjaro had been on his list for years. One of his son's had even done the climb. So, Dave and I, two Safas (South African), decided to convince Andy, another Safa, it was time. *'n Boer maak 'n plan* (a farmer makes plans). I met with Andy mid-August, for lunch at Café 63. By the end of the week, he was in.

Andy has a 'why' story of his own to tell – one I'll leave for him share later. But from our side, it felt like we'd just added someone who truly belonged. This had been on his radar for decades. Of course, Dave needed someone to prank on the trail and Andy copped it… maybe more than he expected. Andy would maybe say he copped too much!

Around that same time, actually just a few days earlier, in late July, I caught up with Peter and Jenny over breakfast. We'd known each other for a few years, originally connecting through a shared interest in property, but the friendship had grown beyond that. As I shared my Kilimanjaro journey they leaned in with curiosity. It didn't take long before they were asking questions and imagining themselves on the trail. They were clearly looking for their next adventure, and didn't need an information night to get there. Their decision came quickly and with it, another level of energy to the group.

Meanwhile, in early August, I caught up with another friend for a sushi lunch. He hadn't been able to make the second information night. Another casual conversation. Another nudge forward. Our group really did start to grow one coffee, one story, one person at a time.

With Andy, Peter and Jenny now on board, we had ten people training together. The momentum was real.

We were now looking at six 'single' tents and two 'couple' tents on the mountain.

But somewhere along the way, on a hike or maybe at an information night, a conversation came up about tent configurations. The idea was simple but important; making sure each climber had their own space to retreat to at night. Couples could decide whether they wanted a shared two-person tent or individual tent for extra space.

It turned out to be a very good call, having our own tents.

Now, Time for Deposits

With our growing crew, I emailed Erasto to confirm we now had ten people. Unreal. Who would've thought it? I asked about the deposit timeline. I didn't want to ask for deposits too early. Momentum was good, but I was still mindful of how easily things can alter.

Zara Tours was happy to receive deposits in early September, about three and a half months ahead of departure. Perfect.

Although there was some chat in the WhatsApp group about timing and payment details, I held off until mid-August to start collecting. By then, we'd already had three group training hikes. Libby even arranged a Brisbane work trip to coincide with one of the hikes in July, an effort that didn't go unnoticed by the group. That hike included a birthday celebration for Moo, organised by Deb.

As it turns out, asking for deposits does more than confirm logistics; it clarifies commitment. There's something about putting money down that silently commits people and moves them from thinking about the idea to owning it. For me, it was a helpful way to see where people were really at. From the initial talking to training and now transfers – it was getting real.

As anticipated, the deposit phase revealed one final unknown: one person wasn't sure they could go. It was helpful to know. We now had nine confirmed, one maybe.

That sparked an interesting conversation: what is the ideal group size?

A few of us started chatting about what makes a good-sized group for an adventure like this. At nine, we weren't too small. But what if it grew?

We agreed that 12 would be our upper limit.

The Final Push

In early October, with three months to go, we made a final group effort to see if there was anyone else keen to join. On the 19th, Belinda and I had coffee with a couple – Amanda and Peter. They joined the next group hike on the 27th and fitted in well. But after working through their decision process, two key factors held them back. As much as they would've loved to come, it just wasn't the right time.

Then came a call from John. He'd heard from Andy (the ongoing ripple effect) what we were doing and was intrigued. It had been a few years since we'd crossed paths, but I knew John, a much-loved school-teacher on the cusp of retiring from full time teaching. He'd recently turned 70 and he wasn't taking it lightly.

What struck me most was his intent; he didn't just want to mark a milestone – he wanted to shake things up. "I don't just want to exist – I want to make sure I'm living," he told me. That resonated with me. We caught up for a coffee and before long, he started coming to group hikes, giving himself a few weeks to test the waters.

By early December, he'd said yes to the mountain.

John was the final addition to the group – and he gave us a fun stat. Before he joined, the median age was below 55. With John on board, we bumped it well over 55. He became a bit of a celebrity on the mountain. Other climbers kept stopping for selfies with him. In particular we noticed that younger Asian climbers wanted a photo of him on the mountain out of respect for what he was doing at his age. John politely obliged each time.

Just after John said yes, we got some disappointing news. Moo didn't receive medical clearance to travel. Still, in true Moo fashion, she kept training with the group. We missed her on the climb, but her presence during training remained a gift.

After our early December group training session, we had ten adventurous souls locked in – committed to meeting in Moshi, Tanzania, on Thursday the 23rd of January 2025, for our final briefing with Festo.

It felt unreal in the best possible way – I was pinching myself.

From that uncertain moment back in early 2024 – when I cautiously told Erasto I might bring 'one or two friends', I was now standing on the edge of this incredible adventure with nine others. It was hard to believe how it had all come together.

Along the way, there had been coffees, info nights, WhatsApp chats, gear debates, birthdays, withdrawals, apologetic cancellations and new additions. And there had been training – lots of it. We weren't just preparing physically. We were bonding. Forming a team.

As I look back, what stands out isn't just that ten of us signed up. It's that everyone had their own story, their own 'why' and their own journey to the decision. And even for those who couldn't come, like Moo, who trained with us anyway, the ripple effect had already taken hold.

This wasn't just about getting to the summit. It was about sharing the path, one step at a time, before we even set foot on the mountain.

We were doing this together. Bring it on!

The Kilimanjaro Decision Funnel

"From Maybe to Mountain" – The 6 Checkpoint Journey

Stage	Question People Ask Themselves	What's Really Happening	Danger Zone Thought
💲 1. Can I afford this?	Gear, flights, visas… oh my.	The reality of the cost is added up – flights etc.	"Maybe I'll do it next year…"
🏃 2. Am I fit enough, and do I want to get fit?	Time to assess the knees.	Hello Google, "training for altitude."	"Do I have to give up wine?"
📅 3. Can I afford to take the time to go?	10+ days away from real life.	Calendars are consulted. Favors called in.	"There's a wedding that weekend…"
👫 4. Will I fit in with this group?	Who *are* these people?	WhatsApp banter is analyzed.	"What if they're morning people?"
🏠 5. What will my family think?	Will family be ok with the risk?	Stories are pitched. Risks are downplayed.	"What if they say no?"
⚠️ 6. Is it safe?	Altitude, cold, unknowns.	Fears meet facts. YouTube gets a workout.	"Is this the one where people freeze?"

Getting to yes is not a straight line. It is a zigzag of enthusiasm, doubt, Google searches and WhatsApp messages. A well-timed info night or casual coffee helps people move forward – one checkpoint at a time.

– Co-authored by Michael Delport and ChatGPT

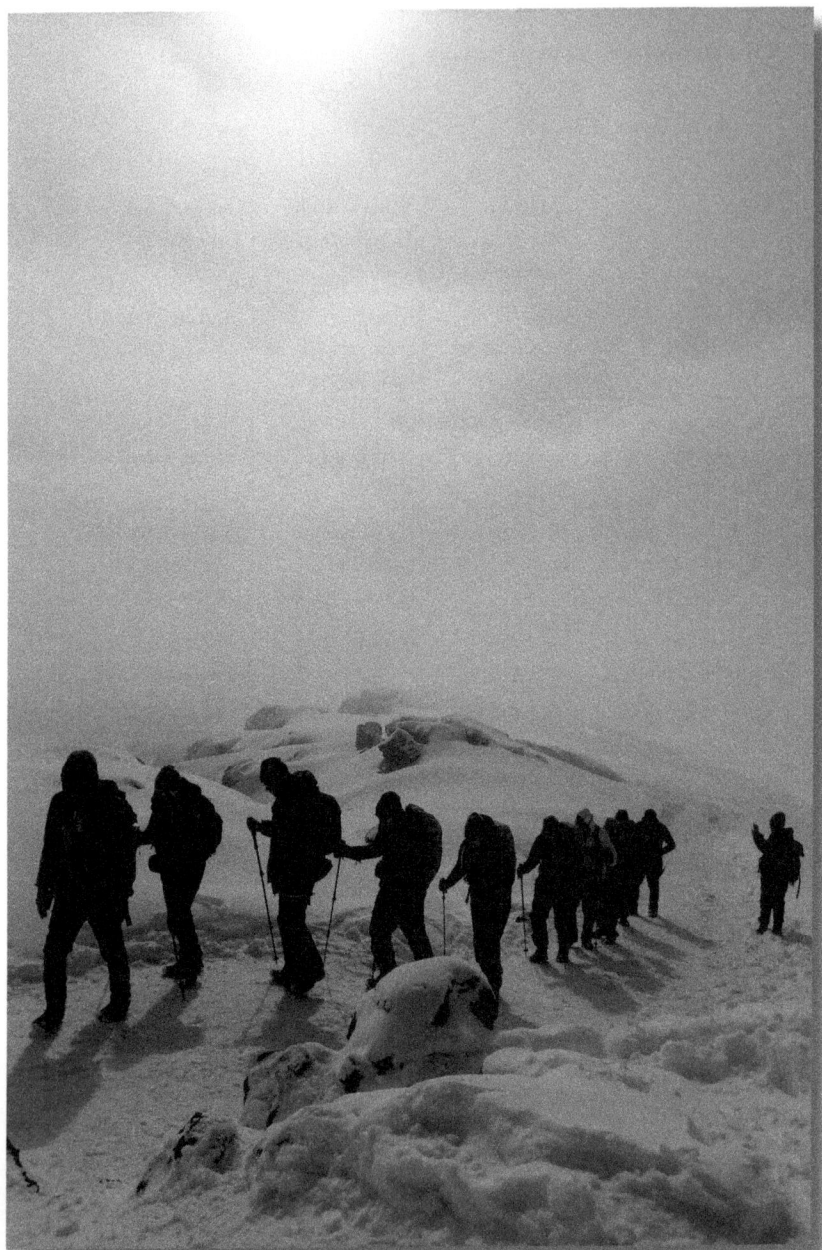

THE CLIMB: WE SUMMIT TOGETHER

"Discipline is the bridge between goals and accomplishment."

– Jim Rohn

CHAPTER EIGHT

❦

TEN DREAMERS, ONE MASSIVE MOUNTAIN

We were doing this. Together. Ten dreamers, one massive mountain. As they say, "It's about the journey, not the destination."

While there's plenty of truth in that, let's be honest – the destination matters. It gives shape to the journey. Without our shared goal of summiting Kilimanjaro, there'd have been no "journey"; no need to train as hard as we did, increase our fitness, clean up the diet, medical check-ups, gear up, squeeze in altitude training, sort out travel logistics, and block time out of our already full calendars. The destination gave us the why behind the effort.

I've said it before, but I'll say it again: it felt like a privilege. A rare one. Everything just seemed to click. There were moments along the way when I'd stop and think, *how is this all coming together so well?* It felt seamless, but of course, it wasn't without effort. That's what made it so meaningful.

I miss it. Not the summit – but the journey. The rhythm of it all. The feeling that we were in it together. You can't go back, but you *can* revisit it. And that's what I'm inviting you to do with me now, across these next three chapters.

The Group Planning

Deb and I naturally stepped into the roles of facilitators for the group. It wasn't formal – we just started checking in with each other every couple of weeks. Sometimes it was a quick phone call, other times it was over coffee when we needed to map things out. Deb brought so much value, especially with her numerous past adventure experiences. She had a real sense for group dynamics – where people were at, what they needed, when to push and when to pause. I genuinely enjoyed teaming up with her.

The WhatsApp group that Deb launched, complete with a few sub-groups, quickly became our training hub. The 'Kili 25 Training' chat took off. Suddenly we were swapping workout ideas, posting our weekly hikes and building momentum. Accountability kicked in and you could feel the enthusiasm growing.

Our first group hike was scheduled for the 30th of June 2024, and I couldn't help but think back to the year before, when it was just me, my sister in Holland and my brother-in-law in South Africa. Back then, we did everything on our own – long walks, swimming, gym, stair climbs, and even gym steppers and yoga. Well… not yoga for me. I do the old man's version, which is basically a traditional Thai massage, where they do the stretching for you.

This time around, the ideas flowed in from everywhere. Saunas. Overnight hikes. Anaerobic bursts to get the heart pumping. Everyone was finding their own way to level up.

The Group Size

When the group size reached nine definite climbers and one maybe, the earlier question about members became more pertinent. What makes for a good-sized group on a challenge like this? At that point, no one was worried the group was too small – nine was solid. The bigger question was what if it kept growing? Should we still cap it at 12? What happens if it creeps up to 15 or even 20?

Together, as touched upon previously, we had landed on a number that felt just right: capping it at 12. Anything between 8 and 12 gave us the best shot at the kind of experience we were all hoping for.

A few reasons stood out:

- **Balance of friendships**: It's big enough for a variety of personalities, but not so big that you miss getting to know each person. With 8 to 12, you've got enough variety in personalities to keep things interesting and supportive.
- **Shared meals**: We all agreed – there's something special about gathering around one long table. On the mountain, we all fitted into a single mess tent. That made a difference. Everyone was in the same conversation. No sub-groups. No one on the outside.
- **Team dynamic**: That size meant there was always someone to encourage you, someone to walk alongside, someone to celebrate a small win with. We weren't just climbing the mountain – we were climbing *together*.
- **Group input and manageability**: Keeping the group small meant we could still make decisions as a group without it turning into chaos. It felt like a conversation, not a committee meeting.

We actually added one more reason to the list – but only after the climb. On summit night, when things got really tough, there was a real discussion about whether we'd need to split the group up. It was a tough but necessary conversation – handled with care.

- **Flexibility on the mountain:** This only became clear during the climb itself. When things got tough, especially on summit night, we had just enough people to support each other while staying agile. If someone needed to slow down, we could adapt.

I've heard stories of larger groups – 15, 18, even 20 people – and they almost always come with the same feedback. Logistics get clunky, meals take longer, hiking pace becomes hard to sync and the connection disappears. You lose that tight-knit feel. On the flip side, too small – less than six – and it gets risky. One person drops out and suddenly there's a gap, both practically and emotionally. It also places more pressure on each team member to keep morale up.

I still remember what it was like for my sister and brother-in-law when I had to pull out the year before. When the group shrunk unexpectedly, everything changed. The two of them ended climbing with Festo and six porters – still a good experience, but not what they'd prepared for.

For us, that sweet spot of 8 to 12 wasn't just a number. It shaped the experience. There was enough diversity of age, strength, life experience, to help carry each other, especially as the altitude kicked in. Just enough to feel like a team and not tourists.

Our very first training hike had six of us. It was the perfect number to rotate through conversations, get to know one another and feel like a team right out of the gate. We never dropped below six after that and, on one memorable occasion, we had a full house – including Libby, who flew up from Melbourne.

The Group training

After the first information night, Deb and I caught up for coffee to talk next steps. One of the big things we needed to figure out was the timing – when to start the group hikes. Based on a few comments in the WhatsApp chat, we pitched a plan to kick off with our first hike at the end of June. We would aim for monthly hikes through the Australian winter and spring, and then, in the final three months before the climb, move it to fortnightly sessions.

The group gave the plan a big thumbs up, so we locked it in. It worked.

We deliberately made the first group hike a relaxed afternoon session followed by a BBQ at Deb and Ken's place. That shared meal afterwards was about more than just the quality steaks Ken cooked for the group. It gave us space to talk, laugh and get to know each other without hiking boots on.

From that moment, we locked in dates for the next four hikes:

- **30th June 2024** – First hike at Mt Cotton, Brisbane with six of us. Plus, Dave and his wife Mel joined us for the BBQ at Deb and Ken's.
- **28th July 2024** – Mt Coot-tha hike planned by Belinda. Eight turned up – Libby flew up from Melbourne and it was Moo's birthday.
- **25th August 2024** – Enoggera Trail, planned by Moo. Another group of six.

- **29th September 2024** – Toohey Forest hike, organised by Peter and Jenny (2 hours). Eight showed up, but I couldn't join as my wife, and I were in Greece for our son Tim's wedding to our beautiful daughter in law Holly.

Before leaving for the wedding, Deb and I locked in the dates for the fortnightly hikes leading into December:

- **12th October 2024** – Mt Coot-tha, facilitated by Belinda (3 hours). Six of us with Libby again flying in from Melbourne. It was incredibly hot, despite an early start. Near the end of the hike, we were all exhausted. Belinda summed it up perfectly – warning us that she had lost her personality. She meant it, but the way she said it had us laughing with understanding. Her presence carried a quiet confidence, as if to say without words: *we can do this, we are going to do this.*
- **16th October 2024 – Zoom Q&A with Michelle.**
  My sister Michelle generously hosted a Zoom call for the group. Having summited Kilimanjaro the year before, she spoke with refreshing honesty. What caught us all off guard was her focus on *the descent* – not the summit. She even got up and demonstrated an exercise for knees and leg strength right there on camera. That visual stayed with us. And then she surprised the ladies by admitting she had cut her own hair on safari, just days before her climb, to make it easier to manage on the mountain. It was practical, no-nonsense Michelle; direct, real and unforgettable.
- **27th October 2024** – Mt Coot-tha again (3 hours). Ten showed up. Two newbies, Amanda and Peter who were still deciding whether to join.

- **9th November 2024** – Mt Gravatt (2.5 hours), planned by Deb and Moo. John joined us for his first hike with the group.
- **24th November 2024** – Springbrook – Pinnacles Peak Loop. A tough one – 5 hours with 1000m of elevation, planned by Andy. Seven turned up for the early 5am meet-up at Macca's.
- **8th December 2024** – Mt Coot-tha again (4 hours), this time planned by me. Eight showed up and our increased fitness was evident.
- **21st December 2024** – Final group hike before Christmas. Mt Coot-tha (just over 3 hours). Nine showed up, Moo included even though she was not joining us on the climb. Dan and Belinda sent their apologies due to Christmas plans.

These hikes gave us two things: the kilometres under our legs that we needed; and, just as importantly, time together. This wasn't just about climbing a mountain – it was about *being* a group. Learning each other's stories, rhythms, strengths. We were preparing for ten days together – eight on the mountain and bookend days at Springlands hotel, sharing space, altitude, challenge and achievement.

Facilitating Hikes

It takes effort to get group hikes going, but even more to keep them going. What I appreciated most is how the responsibility to plan them started to occur naturally. Deb took the lead for the first one, setting the tone with the hike and the BBQ. From there, Belinda, our resident personal trainer, offered to plan the next one. That spontaneous passing of the baton after each hike became the pattern. It made a big difference for Deb and me. We weren't carrying it alone. And it meant we explored a variety of tracks all over the Southeast corner of Queensland.

Seriously, there are some stunning hikes out there. I now have a list of favourite trails I never knew existed. Queensland's hiking scene holds its own.

And while Libby was based in Melbourne, she was no less committed. Training almost entirely on her own in the national parks around Victoria, she posted her Garmin (smartwatch) results on WhatsApp with quiet discipline. Then, on top of that, she still flew to Brisbane to join us for several hikes. That kind of commitment didn't just inspire respect – it raised the bar for the rest of us. Everyone noticed the solo efforts she was putting in down south.

Andy's Hike – 24th November 2024.

Andy had been bringing a measured discipline to the group since he said yes to the mountain. Once he committed, he made the time; fitting in gym sessions, his love for saunas and hikes around his work schedule. He was also a steady support for everyone, looking out for others. That mix of steadiness and discipline made him the perfect one to suggest a hike that would test us.

Somewhere along the way Andy let the group know he had the perfect hike in mind. Decent elevation, solid distance and it would require an early start. He'd done it a few times before and promised it was a challenge – 12 kilometres, three-plus hours and definitely one for walking poles.

We pencilled it in for later in the year, closer to the climb. That timing made sense because we wanted everyone to have a solid fitness base before we took it on.

I couldn't make the scheduled group date, so I did the hike a week earlier on my own. I'll admit, I didn't quite manage Andy's suggested 5am start – I may have allowed myself a sleep-in. But I wanted to fit it into my training and, truthfully, I also wanted to check whether it might be too much for anyone in the group who was still building confidence. The last thing we wanted was for someone to feel discouraged.

Andy and I had talked about this, being sensitive to where each person was at. You could always tell by the heavy breathing on the climbs who was finding it tough. And that was okay. We weren't all at the same starting line. What mattered was supporting each other to keep moving forward.

On the day of the group hike, everyone met at a Mc Donald's at 5am, just south of Brisbane. I'm sure there were a few sleepy faces in the carpark, but plenty of hidden excitement too. The group carpooled to Springbrook, tucked into the hinterland behind the Gold Coast and set off.

Talking with the group afterwards I learnt it didn't take long for them to realise this one was different. The first climb hit hard – 500 metres of elevation right out of the gate. The lungs worked overtime. Poles weren't optional; they were essential. But the timing was perfect. Those who had done several hikes to date were ready for Andy's hike and, for the others, it was a wakeup call.

They knew it was time to put some more hours under their boots, to be 'comfortably ready'. It was not too late, even though there was less than two months to go. John had to dig deep and to his credit he did. He'd only joined the group recently, but I'm sure he'd agree his weekly gym attendance is what got him through.

It wasn't just physical – it was mental. That's what made it so valuable. It gave the group something to draw on later. When things got tough on the mountain, you had the memory bank to call on. *We've done harder. We've pushed through.*

Part of training is building up that memory bank: memories of endurance successes.

That hike ended up being a turning point. It shed light on the way the group saw their preparedness and how much training we were doing. From then on, the early starts didn't feel quite so outrageous.

Andy even offered to lead a few more at 5am.

And yes – people showed up – by then we were committed.

Training Schedule – Did It Work?

I can say with confidence now that the way we structured our group hikes worked. It wasn't just about building physical fitness and building the group dynamics. It was also about individual mindsets.

That Springbrook hike set the tone; but really, all of them added something. When you've got a few tough hikes under your belt, they become more than just training sessions. As I explained they become memories you can pull from when you're struggling.

For me, one of those memories returned when climbing in the Drakensberg on Day Two with Anton and my nephews. It was tough – we were hauling 15 kilo packs up a brutal 1,200-metre ascent. Raw, steep and relentless. To get through it, I found myself reaching back to another difficult climb I'd done before, calling on that memory as proof that I could push through again. The rasp of our breathing, the burn in the legs, the dust underfoot – it all came with the same inner dialogue: *you're done… no, you're not. Keep going.*

I also noticed a definite willingness to start hikes earlier – especially as the weather warmed up. At the beginning, the idea of hitting the trail before 7am felt like a stretch. Honestly, a bit of a joke for some of us (me included). But as we pushed forward, 6am starts became the new normal. Then 5am didn't sound quite so crazy anymore.

It wasn't just a shift in the calendar – it was a shift in our thinking. A shift in what we knew we'd need to do on the mountain.

That's what Kilimanjaro demands. It's not just about long walks. It's walking for hours, sometimes in the dark, sometimes uphill, sometimes while your body is screaming at you to stop. We needed that mental edge just as much as the physical one.

The group hikes were the highlights, for sure, but they were also checkpoints. Everyone was training in between. The group hikes gave us a shared rhythm, but each person was also putting in the solo work – gym, sauna, swimming, hill repeats, stairs and more.

So, over time, something else happened: we became a team. When you spend a few hours hiking side-by-side with someone, you talk about more than the weather. You hear about families, jobs, challenges, and dreams. You shuffle walking positions, and, by the end of a few hikes, you've rubbed shoulders with everyone. By Christmas, we weren't just individuals trying to tick off a bucket-list mountain. We were a proper team.

We floated the idea of one more group hike before flying out, but the calendar got tight because of Christmas, New Year and people leaving on different dates. In the end, we left it up to each person to squeeze in what they could. A few of us had altitude time, or solo training planned. But what we'd already done together had laid the groundwork.

We were ready.

Personal Progress

I still remember that first group hike in June, it felt like a slap in the face. A real wake-up call. We were out in the Cleveland area, east of Brisbane, nothing too serious. Maybe three kilometres up to a lookout, then back down again. Five or six kilometres in total. I'd done much longer hikes in the past, but this one hit differently.

Six months since my surgery. Including three months of barely doing anything. It all caught up with me on that first incline.

I'd been walking here and there. Swimming. Even getting back into the pool felt like progress. But that hike was the first time I'd felt how much fitness I'd actually lost. There was just enough elevation to expose it. I was puffed. I was slower. I felt every extra kilo I'd put on. The scales were back up in the high 90s – five or six more than the year before when I was fit and ready for the first climb.

Now? I was nowhere near that. *Ag, nie. Ek is nie gereed nie!* (Oh, no. I'm not ready!).

But it was what I needed. That hike reminded me of that brutal truth: you don't get up Kilimanjaro on good intentions. I knew I'd have to ramp things up between our group sessions if I wanted to be ready for the next hike; which would be a longer, harder one, just a few weeks away.

So, I went back to the basics. I pulled out the same routine I'd followed in 2023. Swimming twice a week. Walking often. Some gym work – though let's be honest, mostly for the sauna. No squash, not yet. I didn't want to risk an injury. That part of the routine hadn't made its way back in after the operation. But I was moving. I was building again.

Week by week, the laps in the pool increased. The hikes got longer. The weights got heavier. And bit by bit, that magic feeling returned – that sense of momentum, of doing something hard and getting better at it. There's nothing quite like it. I love that feeling.

By Christmas, I was feeling good. Not perfect. But ready. One month out from the climb, I had one last piece to fit in – my altitude prep. Something personal. Something special.

Something I came to call the *'Uncle Michael Weekend'*.

Uncle Michael Weekend.

As part of my training, I rang my brother-in-law, Anton, with an idea. "I've been thinking," I said. "What do you reckon about doing something together in South Africa before I head to Tanzania? We missed out last year on being on Kilimanjaro together. How about we make up for it? Let's get on a mountain together."

He was all in.

I suggested a hike in the Drakensberg Mountains, somewhere with altitude – above 3,000 metres if possible. I told him I'd be flying via South Africa to Tanzania, spending a bit of time with extended family there and then heading off to Tanzania for my second attempt. I was keen to fit in some proper altitude time and a three-day hike felt like just the thing.

Anton got to work searching for the right trail. He found a beauty – a route on the northern edge of Lesotho, right along the border with South Africa. We locked it in. The 17th to 19th of January, just a week before I'd be standing at the base of Kilimanjaro again.

And then came the surprise – his two sons, Joubert and Riaan, decided to join us. My brother, Anton thought about coming too, along with his son Ruben. In the end, my brother couldn't make it, but Ruben did! Suddenly, it wasn't just a hike – it was a family adventure. Me, my brother-in-law and three nephews. It felt like something out of a movie.

Over three days, we covered 45 kilometres. Each of us carried our own gear – packs weighing 15 kilos or more, loaded with food, sleeping bags, and tents – the lot. It was raw and real. Exactly the kind of challenge I'd hoped for. One of those magic moments that only happen when something goes 'wrong' in life first. If I'd summited Kilimanjaro the year before, this trip never would've happened. But I hadn't – and this one did. I'm so glad it did.

There's one photo from that hike that has fond memories. On the family WhatsApp. Holly noted that the five of us looked like extras from the Jumanji movie so – messy, muddy, totally in our element. Riaan even edited the photo to look like a movie poster – it became the unofficial trip picture. Then there was Riaan's prank – sneaking a heavy rock into his brother's backpack after the big 1,200 metre ascent. It stayed there for an hour until we stopped to set up camp in a cave and the truth came out. That laugh was worth the effort.

Evenings brought their own rhythm – cooking, laughter, stories and of course, a game of Canasta. That card game seems to travel with our family wherever we go. But it was the conversations that stayed with me. Especially one about neurodiversity. My three nephews, all thoughtful and articulate, shared their views on learning differences and education. I mostly listened. I've known I was dyslexic since primary school so, hearing them speak so insightfully about the topic, struck a chord.

What moved me most, though, was something simple. For those three days, I kept on hearing – "Uncle Michael." Over and over. And that meant something.

I come from a big family – six siblings living across five different countries. Between us, we've got 13 nieces and nephews. But time with them? Proper, unhurried time? That's rare. For those three days, I wasn't just training for a mountain. I was their uncle.

And I'll always be grateful for that.

It was time – Training Was Up

On the 22nd of January, I left Joburg and boarded my Air Tanzania flight via Dar es Salaam to Moshi. I touched down at Kilimanjaro Airport at

11pm. It was late and I was tired, but I felt ready. I'd chosen this route deliberately – I wanted to be there from the very start on the 23rd of January, when the rest of the group was due to arrive at Springlands Hotel. Everyone had their own travel plans, arriving at different times. Some were already in Tanzania, getting in a bit of altitude time or rest before the climb.

For me, this was it.

This was the moment I'd missed a year earlier.

This time, **I was sure I was going to be on the bus to Londorossi Gate,** the start of the Lemosho Route.

"Life is either a daring adventure
or nothing at all."

– Helen Keller

CHAPTER NINE

TANZANIA, TAKE TWO: THE
SUMMIT. THE DESCENT.
THE CELEBRATIONS

Déjà Vu, I was back in Tanzania.

On the flight from Joburg to Kilimanjaro, I felt that familiar nervous excitement churning in my gut. Everything I'd been preparing for – the original training, the surgery setbacks, the re-training, and the relentless drive to get back – was about to be tested. Two years of planning, recovery and determination, had all led to this. I was back to finish what I'd started – and this time, with a group of adventurous friends.

My flight touched down late at night, just before 11pm. Unlike my first visit, I didn't get to see the grand silhouette of the mountain from the plane. Still, the familiarity hit hard. Kilimanjaro Airport hadn't changed a bit. I knew where to go. The odd post-flight baggage scan, the ATM tucked awkwardly in the corner and the Zara Tours rep holding a placard with my name. It all felt slightly surreal – like slipping back into a dream that had been on pause.

I checked into Springlands Hotel, just before midnight, on the 22nd of January 2025 and collapsed into bed. Tomorrow, I'd reconnect with the rest of the group as they trickled in throughout the day. I was eagerly anticipating the moment when we'd all be assembled for our afternoon briefing with Festo.

Festo's Briefing Session

It was genuinely good to see Festo again. I'm not sure he was expecting a big bear hug, but being who he is, he embraced it warmly. He remembered exactly who I was, what I'd been through and even recollected helping my sister and brother-in-law summit. Impressive, when you think about how many climbers, he's led up that mountain! This is his career. He's lost count of his summits. To say we were in good hands is an understatement. Festo is exceptional.

He spent a couple of hours with the ten of us; introducing his core team, giving an overview of the eight-day climb, checking dietary needs, and confirming hired gear and reviewing our summit night equipment. Then came the glamourous bit – Portaloos. For the uninitiated, imagine a compact toilet inside a small, private tent that is carried up the mountain and set up by the porters at each campsite. One was included, but did we want a second? We agreed to have two; one for the lads, one for the ladies.

And of course, there were plenty of questions. How could there not be? We were sitting there with the mountain looming in the background and each of us wondering: *Would I make it?* The climb ahead was real. We helped each other mentally walk through our four to eight months of preparation. What to wear each day, what to pack in our duffels (15kg limit), what to carry in daypacks, tent configurations (six tents for singles, two for couples) and what to expect regarding painkillers, malaria tablets, Diamox, water purification – you name it. We were all doing a final mental check. Quietly assessing risk. And mentally suiting up.

Kilimanjaro isn't Everest, with its death zone, but it's not your average Sunday hike either. Around three to 10 people die each year attempting it. The causes? Altitude illnesses like HAPE and HACE, pre-existing heart conditions, accidents from falls or rockslides, and sudden hypothermia from rapid weather changes.

Festo took time to memorize all our names and a detail or two about each of us. He already knew Andy and Dave, having guided them up Mt Meru, just days prior, for their altitude training. A significant climb in its own right. They shared stories of their three-day hike, and we got our first taste of Dave's ongoing pranks. Every group has a scallywag, and I love it. There's always someone who reminds us that adventure doesn't mean leaving humour behind.

The briefing ended well. A great first dinner together, then we all headed to bed thinking about last-minute packing – and a last good sleep in a real bed before our long-awaited start.

On the Bus

Wow! The morning I'd been waiting for had finally arrived. This time, I was *on* the bus – not watching it leave without me.

I made a point of soaking it all in. Unlike Festo who had done these many times before, this wasn't familiar terrain for me. This was the adventure I'd had on my radar for more than three decades and, for two years, one I had fully committed to. It was happening. And I was present for every moment.

That sense of awareness wasn't just mine. Across the ten days together, I saw it come and go in all of us – little moments where someone paused to take it all in. Between us, we ended up with over 500 photos and 80 videos. We knew this was a once-in-a-lifetime experience.

Being on the bus brought back memories of watching my sister and brother-in-law leave 14 months earlier while I stayed behind. This time, I was headed with the group to Londorossi Gate at 2,250 metres. It was the start of the Lemosho Route in the northern section of Kilimanjaro National Park, which spans a vast 1,688 square kilometres.

The two-hour bus ride was a silent reflection for many of us. I could see how people were managing their thoughts in different ways. There was a buzz; nervous excitement, not exactly spoken but definitely felt. Like that feeling before a parachute jump – only with a longer lead-up. And Kilimanjaro? She was there the whole way, rising on the right side of the bus. No hiding from her size.

John, up front, was composing lyrics for what he called 'The Diamox Blues', inspired by the altitude meds and their side effects. I never did hear the final version, but the image of him scribbling away added something quirky to the mix.

There were the necessary pit stops alongside the road and a small town where Festo needed to stop for supplies. In a two-hour trip, there was more than one break. Diamox was clearly doing its job. The rest of us drifted between chatting and falling into quiet observation. We were all thinking about the climb. You could feel it.

Personally, I just wanted the walk to begin – to shift from all the build-up into actually doing it. A bit like public speaking. I don't mind it, but even after doing it a few times, the nerves still come. This felt similar.

The best cure, I knew, was to just begin. It was time. I needed to take the first step.

We were off the bus and on the mountain by the afternoon of Friday, the 24th of January 2025. And immediately, we hit what my sister had described perfectly: the *hurry up and wait*. Just like the familiar feeling you get at airports – rush to get in line, only to sit and wait. There was a rush to line up for a compulsory check-in at the ranger's hut – but then we waited. We could see the trail just ahead and were itching to get going. Instead, we tucked into packed lunch boxes, applied sunscreen, took photos and used the last 'normal' toilets before heading out. Festo's team of porters had to leave first to set up camp before our arrival. Zara Tours was a well-oiled operation under his leadership.

Now, I won't bore you with a blow-by-blow of my mini mountain journal – the one I kept each night, as did a few others among us. But there are moments that stand out – milestones and memories that stitched those eight days together into something unforgettable.

Personally, I experienced the mountain in three distinct phases: the acclimatisation journey to base camp; summit night; and the descent. Each with its own pace, vibe, challenge and reward.

The Climb to Base Camp

Eventually, we all stood at the trailhead, daypacks on, waiting out 15 long minutes for the call to start. We weren't quite pacing, but I was circling the start, ready to move. No one wanted to be the one who said it out loud: "Can we go now?" Then finally, the call came. We were off – three and a half hours of gentle climbing ahead. Just enough time to reach the first stop, Mt Mkubwa Camp (Big Tree camp), before sunset.

Some of us had the route details saved on our mobile phones; distances, elevation changes, terrain types. We knew the plan for the eight days and regularly checked it to stay mentally prepared for what each stage would demand of us.

But what a plan can't prepare you for is how the mountain makes you *feel*. Would we all summit? How would we cope with the altitude, the weather, each other? The numbers were helpful, but the real journey unfolded one breath, one conversation, one moment at a time.

The climb to base camp split into a rhythm – *'pole pole'* (slowly slowly). Those first six days and five nights were about acclimatisation. Ten people adjusting to altitude, soaking up the mountain, occasional laughter, quiet chats, managing gear, watching weather and building something unspoken between us.

Festo kept reminding the lead guide, Geoffrey, to slow down, even though to us, it already felt like we were walking slowly. At first, it was hard to adjust. Back home, I'd trained at a pace of one kilometre every 10 to 15 minutes, depending on elevation. On Kilimanjaro, it was closer to 30 to 60 minutes per kilometre. A crawl by comparison – but that's what it was about.

"Pole Pole" became the new norm. Slowly, slowly. It didn't take long to stop resisting the slowness. You slip into the rhythm and start to trust it. Your body is doing what it needs to do – acclimatising. And more importantly, you trust that Festo knows what he's doing. He's reading the mountain. Reading us. Every slow step is part of the strategy. Not a delay, but a decision.

Every day, the mountain reminded us it wasn't to be taken lightly. Helicopters overhead – sometimes one, sometimes two – became a normal part of the soundscape. On Day 2, climbing Elephant Back *en route* to Shira 1 Camp, we heard a chopper through the trees. Sobering. Someone else's bad day. A reminder of what was at stake.

That was the thing about Kilimanjaro – it demanded respect, but it also invited reflection. The same trail that triggered anxiety for one person could spark stillness in another.

It was near the top of the Elephant Back that I noticed a change in Dan. That was where the last bars of phone reception vanished, cutting him off from his international corporate world. Unreachable at last, he surprised me by stopping to photograph the mountain's small details, and something I don't do well. With no emails able to reach him, he began to relax into the climb, a gentle smile on his face, simply enjoying the moment. He was where he wanted to be, where he needed to be.

I'd heard stories from years past about rubbish being a real problem on Kilimanjaro – scraps left behind, campsites untidy. But credit where it's due: today the mountain is impressively well-kept. The rangers and trekking crews have worked hard to change that culture and you notice it straight away. Even so, Peter and Jenny took it one step further. Without fuss, they picked up the odd piece of litter along the trail and carried it down with them – a simple act of respect for the mountain that spoke volumes about who they were.

Still, the highlights were unforgettable. Elephant Back's rugged terrain. The fantastic mess tent tea at Lava Tower (4,600m), served in falling snow. Or the mighty Barranco Wall – intimidating from below, with no clear path visible. But we climbed it together, step by step, helping each other through. That was more than physical – it was a team moment.

It was on difficult sections of the climbs that Peter's strength showed itself most clearly. He never drew attention to it, but you could see it in the way he supported Jenny and others when the going got tough. Steady, solid and selfless, he carried his strength without fuss – and that was when he truly became better known to us. Jenny was observant and quick to offer help, whether it was passing me my water bottle from the side pocket of my backpack, or calling "Porters coming through!" as the long lines of porters moved past, making sure we stepped aside in timely manner.

Managing your body temperature became part of the daily routine – just another challenge layered into the climb. With the gradual increase in altitude and any weather changes, there was the daily decision of what to wear. How many layers? How many socks? By Day 6, getting dressed felt like prepping for battle. Thermals, hiking trousers, long-sleeved shirts, fleeces, two pairs of socks, worn-in boots, gloves ready, puffers, sunscreen. Then came the layers dance – on again, off again. Zips down, zips up. Hands in, hands out. You were constantly regulating your body temp based on altitude, weather and effort.

Our Energizer bunny, Dave, had a way of throwing himself into things with restless energy – sometimes chaotic, often funny. But just when you needed it most, he'd surprise you. After one drenching day, he somehow managed to dry out half the group's gear inside the mess tent, turning misery into relief and appreciation. Unpredictable, inventive, but always there when it mattered.

At night, the same ritual repeated – only more so. With temperatures dropping and the summit approaching, I added layers climbing into my -5 to -15 degree sleeping bag. The night before summit night, I wore thermals, multiple tops, head and ear warmers and even tucked hand warmers between double socks. I managed two hours of actual sleep that night – not everyone did.

But amidst all that layering and logistics, there were moments of stillness I'll never forget.

One that stands out? was the afternoon at Karanga Camp, the night before base camp. I pulled a deck chair from the mess tent and set it outside for a silent moment alone. My tent was ready, sleeping bag rolled out, bowl of hot water ready for my 'bird bath'. I sat there, around 4000 meters above sea level, looking down at Moshi – 3,000 metres below me – and behind me, completely unobstructed, the snow-summit. No clouds. Another 1,900 metres to go. It was just me, the mountain and the space in between. Grounding, dreamlike, unforgettable.

There were lighter milestones too. Like celebrating Australia Day (26 Jan) mid-trek with Libby's Tim Tams and Deb's Vegemite and Minties. Far from our land Down Under, it felt good to share a taste of home on the mountain and the group enjoyed finding small ways to mark the day together. I caught myself wishing I had also thought of something to bring for the moment.

And Dan and Belinda's wedding anniversary, marked somewhere above 4,000 metres – not exactly candlelit, but memorable all the same. Belinda (or Dan) might not have had the candles, but she carried herself with quiet resilience and resourcefulness. She was our backpack magician. What she had with her, just in case, was amazing. Tape, medication, snacks, knee straps, electrolytes – she seemed to have thought of everything.

Then came Deb's birthday two days later. I remember the morning clearly, lying in my tent at 5am, with the sound of snoring in the distance (not mine this time). I heard footsteps outside. "Is that you, Deb?" I called. "Yes," came the reply. "Happy birthday!" I called.

Nicknamed "the Turtle" by her fellow outriggers for always crossing the finishing line, no matter how long it takes. Later that day, the porters honoured her with a round of singing at morning tea and we all joined in. In true Festo style, he'd secretly arranged a delayed cake celebration for the next day.

And then there was Festo. The quiet force at the centre of it all. Calm. Steady. Always watching. You couldn't miss his leadership – not because it was loud, but because it was *constant*. Present.

Each evening before dinner, he'd gather us for a check-in – sometimes brief, sometimes longer. He wasn't just asking how we were; he was scanning. Reading body language. Listening for signs of altitude sickness – headaches, nausea, dizziness, diarrhoea. Subtle things that could derail someone's summit chances. Festo's assistant leaders – Geoffrey, Monday and Mickey – were usually by his side, taking oxygen readings and checking vital signs.

But it wasn't just about physical health. Festo knew this climb was mental. He'd sit with us and ask, "How are you really going?" He was tuning in, adjusting his read on each person. Helping us get in the right headspace. Building belief. Building momentum. He wasn't just leading a trek – he was engineering a chance for each of us to succeed.

And the food! We ate well. Really well. Festo told us how he'd courted the chef for several seasons before convincing him to join the team. His soups became legendary. What that man could produce in a tent kitchen still amazes me. And it made a difference. You don't summit without calories. Or encouragement.

Team Reflections – Climb to Base Camp

Jenny
Amazing scenery and a wide range of vegetation with excellent company and guides. Due to the fact I had eleven pins in my shoulder from a fall off a ladder on an army exercise 10 months earlier, I had to stop on average every 4kms for Pete to massage my shoulders, so I could keep functioning. Apart from one bout of nausea in the sleet and snow, the climb to base camp was outstanding.

Peter

Spectacular, diverse, breathtakingly beautiful and at times certainly challenging. These are some of the adjectives and phrases I would use to describe my trek to base camp on Mt Kilimanjaro. Apart from the natural beauty of the climb, which was significant, the ascent to base camp was enriched by the good humour camaraderie and support so clearly and uniquely provided by every member of the climbing group. To everyone I extend my sincere thanks and gratitude for being able to share this unique experience with them.

Belinda

On the hike, a thought-provoking question was posed to us: which animal do we most identify with? It took me a moment to consider; however, I chose the chameleon. I admire the chameleon's ability to blend into its surroundings, remaining inconspicuous, yet capable of changing its colours when necessary. This metaphor resonated with my experience on Kilimanjaro, as I navigated the various challenges of the hike.

Throughout the journey, I maintained a state of relaxation while staying alert to my environment, adapting physically, mentally and socially to ensure I was in the best position to reach the summit.

Deb

Colobus monkeys flashing their silky tails. A thunderous Barranco avalanche. Scaling the Barranco Wall with views of the plains. A hailstorm at Lava Tower where Festo had a mess tent waiting, just in time. Nights lit by Moshi town below and constellations above.

Mid-trail, I was serenaded by the porters with a jubilant "Happy Birthday." At base camp came another song – Miley Cyrus's *"The Climb."* BOOM – WHOOSH. The emotional floodgates opened. Out gushed the backwaters of stored hurts from the past four years – anxiety that had paralyzed me, prompted me to leave my job, kept me housebound and dimmed any hope of future adventures. Yet despite that paralysis, I chose to adopt someone else's dream. I chose to train daily for 11 months to be here. This was my mountain – and I had already summited it. Whatever I achieved tomorrow would be icing on the cake. My victory cake.

SUMMIT NIGHT

Who decides to get up before midnight after just a few hours of sleep, with dinner still settling and snow falling – only to climb more than 1,200 metres through the night to the highest free-standing mountain in the world?

Well, over 95 percent of Kilimanjaro climbers do. And, on the 29th of January 2025, so did we.

The reason? Timing. The ground is firmer in the cold, the weather more stable and the payoff of reaching Uhuru Peak at sunrise, is both practical and poetic. Festo made the call for us to leave early, around 10pm, knowing our group size and pace. Most groups leave closer to midnight, but he wanted us ahead of the rush and safely down before the heat and wind picked up.

Back in my tent, I geared up, going through my mental checklist. Legs: thermals and hiking trousers. Torso: thermals, snug t-shirt, hiking shirt. Feet: three pairs of socks, toe warmers, waterproof boots. Head: ear and neck warmers. Outerwear: ski pants, puffer, ski jacket with hood. Gloves: two pairs. Backpack packed: 4 litres of water, painkillers, gels, Snickers bars, trail mix, sunscreen, and an extra thermal layer. Poles were clipped to the outside – I prefer not to use them unless necessary.

Even my water bottles were prepped – camel pack to drink first, two bottles turned upside down with socks over them to prevent freezing. Mobile in a zip lock bag in my jacket. I was ready. At least, I thought I was.

Fifteen minutes before departure, I faced an unexpected dilemma. The hired yellow ski bib pants, which I'd only tried on briefly at the hotel and yes, they looked *lekker* (good) in a photo, suddenly felt restrictive. The shoulder straps were stiff. Movement was awkward. With the group about to start, I had to decide risk it or leave them behind. I chose to hike with just two leg layers. I'd skied with less and it had always been fine.

But I wasn't skiing. And Kilimanjaro had its own ideas and personality.

Not long after we set off, passing waves of tents across multiple rocky levels, I could already tell something wasn't right. My thighs were cold. The rest of me felt warm and fine, but that creeping cold on my legs began gnawing at my focus.

Still, I said nothing. We moved in tight formation, headlamps lighting a zigzag trail up the pitch-black mountainside. Earlier that evening, I'd flipped through the ranger logbook, counting climbers – 15 pages, 14 names per page, people from at least ten countries. Over 200 climbers were ascending that night.

Some had set off before us. I looked up at the string of headlamps. Stunning. A line of lights, like a ski slope lit up for night skiing – only this time, the movement was uphill stretching into the snow clouds. But none of us took a photo. That alone says a lot – we were all dealing with our own internal challenges.

It was time to *Vasbyt* (Afrikaans for: grin and bear it, hang on, don't give up).

I tried to distract myself. I began mentally rehearsing the Japanese Hiragana alphabet – its symbols, sounds and sequence. It worked. A couple of hours passed in that mind game.

But by around 2am, someone called out, "We've done 400 metres!"

Wait – 400? That meant we still had 800 metres of elevation still to go.

My legs were now properly cold. Not surface cold – *deep* cold. Hypothermia-level concern. I remembered something my sister had told me before the trip: "Look after yourself first. Don't worry about being an inconvenience." That thought gave me permission to act.

I spoke up.

Festo reacted immediately. He had me sit on a rock and carefully supervised as I took off my boots – keeping my feet lifted so they wouldn't hit the snow. I added a second thermal layer, pulled my trousers back on and before I could lace up again, Festo handed me his own rain trousers.

"Put these on too," he insisted. "I won't need them."

Now four layers deep, I immediately felt warmer. The process took ten minutes. The group had to keep moving – stopping for too long up there isn't safe. The body needs to keep moving to stay warm, even if it's *'pole pole'*. So, we increased pace to catch them. Festo checked in a few times to make sure I was okay. I was. And I was so glad I'd remembered Michelle and spoken up.

It took us over thirty minutes to catch the tail of the group – who were only about 25 metres higher in elevation. That says it all. We were gaining maybe 100 metres an hour. All due to the thin air. No Sunday afternoon stroll!

We were a full group again; ten climbers, plus Festo and assistant leaders. Festo drifted to the back to scan the team, watching body language and facial expressions, always reading the situation. It was around 3am. We'd been climbing for five hours and past the halfway mark to Stella Point, the crater edge.

My thighs were warm now. I'd include them in my mental scans – head to toe, checking in with each part of my body like a pilot doing system checks. Still, I needed a mental distraction. I returned to the Japanese alphabet. Then I moved on to another exercise; recalling every business idea I'd journaled during the climb so far. New ways to improve the trek experience, equipment suggestions, maybe even a better gear list. One I added that night, snow clip-ons for boots. Andy had a pair, which he said was a "game-changer" for him.

By around 6am, the sky began to lighten. It was sunrise, but we hadn't yet reached the crater rim. Even with cloud cover, the path ahead was more visible now, the summit ridge glowing faintly ahead of us. It looked near – maybe 600 to 800 metres along the snow-covered pathway – but it still took another 90 minutes to reach.

We all felt the altitude. Breathing was harder. Twice, I had to pause for a deeper, diaphragm-level breath. It wasn't panic – but it was a reminder. The stretch to Stella Point was steep, winding, relentless.

And then – we arrived.

It was just before 8am. All ten of us reached Stella Point together. Joy. Relief. Exhaustion. But no celebrations like you see at sea level. No one jumped. We barely managed a group photo. It was hard to find the energy to smile. Thin air humbles you. It was an effort to stand still.

Festo gave us space to decide who would keep going. For those who felt completely spent, this was still a massive achievement. And we trusted him to help each person make the call. He knew, who still had something left in the tank. In the end, three of our group began the descent with Monday, one of the assistant guides. Seven of us stayed on to push for the top.

Uhuru Peak was still 139 metres higher and 1.2 kilometres away. Geoffrey led the way. The slope eased slightly and while the pace was steady, it felt more manageable than the final haul we'd just completed to Stella.

Along the way, we passed a few descending groups. They smiled, encouraged us, said, "Not far now," though it still took just over an hour. That's the summit paradox – so close, yet still so far.

And then, at last, we were there.

Uhuru Peak. 5,895 metres above sea level. Highest point in Africa. We stood beneath that iconic weathered wooden sign: *'Congratulations. You are now at Uhuru Peak, Tanzania, 5895m.'*

The weight of the two years finally lifted – you could feel it happening. The wondering was over. There were hugs. Quiet tears. Disbelief. Relief. And photos – so many photos.

I made it! I really made it!

In that moment, it wasn't just about altitude – it was about everything that had brought me here. The setbacks. The surgery. The training. The family. The friendships. The mountain.

The whole journey – the last two years!

We stayed up there for nearly an hour – longer than expected. Not rushing. Just being. We could feel the sun through the clouds, warming our cheeks and burning any exposed skin. But no one was in hurry to leave.

It was about being present. About standing in the place, we'd only imagined from afar. The moment didn't need narrating. It just needed living.

Team Reflections – The Summit

Libby

The excitement and nerves started to build as we got closer to base camp. It was wet, snowy and packed with people. Altitude, noise and adrenaline made sleep elusive. After a late supper we climbed slowly and steadily. Breathing, walking, drinking from my backpack bladder and blowing air back into the tube to keep it from freezing took all my focus and energy. I was really surprised and relieved when the new day came. Festo told me, 'You're going to make it,' and I knew in my heart that I could. The mid-morning sun brightened the already snowy summit. Elation. Exhaustion.

Jenny

For 9 hours, in the darkness and snow it was just literally putting one foot in front of the other and trying to ignore the constant nausea and dizziness, which was compounded by broken climbing poles.

Peter

I was quite surprised by the speed at which a wave of nausea enveloped me on the fourth day of our climb at an elevation of approximately 4600m and even more grateful at how quickly it dissipated after emptying my stomach in the snow that had been quietly accumulating around us during our ascent. I suspect it was also aided by the anti-nausea medication generously provided by Dr Pocock at the time. ☺

Prior to summit evening there had been a couple of occasions where I had been able to provide some level of both physical and emotional support for my wife. Unfortunately, I was able to offer a semblance of emotional encouragement during the summit ascent. My ability to provide any physical help was almost non-existent due to the fatigue I was experiencing due to the elevation. Had it not been for the steady assistance of Mickey, one of our guides helping my wife, I am not sure whether I would have successfully scaled the summit of this magnificent monolith.

Belinda

The most significant takeaway from this experience was the power of positivity. With a resilient mindset and a willing body, the possibilities truly become endless.

Deb

1100m in 9 hours – grueling, grand, epic, brutal. Mind games. Heavy legs. Nosebleeds. Oxygen deprivation. No appetite. Yet with Monday's (my summit guide) assistance, I dug deep – again and again. I pressed on. We eventually reached Stella Point (5756m). I told Festo this would be my turning point. He agreed. My only regret: in the chaos of other groups arriving and our team preparing for the next phase, I missed getting an individual photo at this incredible location. But it is etched in memory – a defining moment I will draw on for future adventures.

Andy

(Here is Andy's why story talked about in Chapter 7

Over three decades ago, a close friend and I decided to climb Mount Kilimanjaro. We lived in Africa, so the idea of climbing the continent's highest mountain seemed quite reasonable. We were young and fit and had had many adventures together, but this was going to be the biggest of them all.

Unfortunately, fate had its own agenda, and we were never to climb the mountain together. Chaos broke out in Zimbabwe and within a few short years my best friend Steffen was living back in South Africa while I had immigrated to Australia. The dream was still there, but it had been postponed. Worse, the dream was dashed when Steffen developed a brain tumour and died within a year. I lost my best friend and our adventures together ended.

Somehow the idea and desire to climb Kilimanjaro never went away. It lived beneath the surface and every time I heard someone climbing the lofty mountain, something inside me felt that I had unfinished business.

About twenty years ago, my eldest son and a close friend of his decided to climb Kilimanjaro. They were young, strong and fit. They both successfully reached the summit but described the climb as one of the hardest things they had ever done. For the first time I wondered whether I had what it took to get to the top. Decades passed and the dream grew dull but never disappeared. The invitation from Michael came out of the blue – a simple question: 'Would you like to join the group climbing Kilimanjaro in January?' No pressure, no hard sell, just an invitation. I knew this was it: now or never. I accepted the invitation, joined the group and started training.

As the climb drew closer, my mind often went back to my dear friend and our unfinished business. I wanted him somehow to be a part of the journey. My wife Jane found some photos of us together and laminated them. Each evening during the climb I took the photos out, thought of him and remembered our friendship. At the summit I held a photograph of him. Imperfect – yes, but in some strange way it felt as if we had made it to the top.

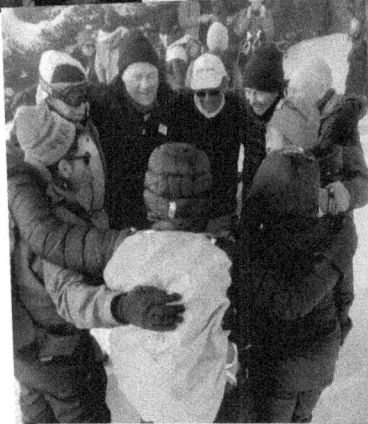

THE DESCENT

What came next? None of us were prepared for it. Even with the Netherland's Information Night, YouTube videos and our conversations with other climbers, nearly 3,000 metres of descent in one day. Yes, gravity helps. But after summiting at 5,895 metres, getting down to our final camp at 2,800 metres took 10 to 12 hours. And it hurt.

The descent came in three brutal sections:

Summit to Base Camp: We took a different route down from the zigzag climb – loose lava scree, dusty and slippery. It felt endless. Our legs screamed, our knees buckled. We arrived at base camp about three hours later, thighs burning and joints aching. Every step was a test.

Base Camp to the 'Past' Camp: This part lulled us into a false sense of ease. A gentle trail through alpine desert, not overly steep – but the drop-in altitude played tricks on our bodies. It was easier to breathe, but fatigue had set in. Our pace quickened, but concentration lagged.

Final Stretch to Mweka Camp: This was the worst. A jarring trail of irregular stone and concrete steps with no rhythm – neither natural nor well-constructed. It punished tired legs and pounded knees. I added it to my mental business list – close this section off, rebuild it, or don't let climbers and porters use it.

Somewhere in all of that, I remembered Michelle's odd advice from a Zoom call four months earlier: "Make sure you include an exercise in your training to help your knees for the descent."

At the time, it felt like a strange opening line. After that descent, it made perfect sense.

Tackling the descent, we were no longer a group of ten. Three had started their return from Stella Point and the seven who reached Uhura ended up splitting up after we passed back through. By late morning, closer to midday, we regrouped briefly at Base Camp. But by then, each of us was handling the descent in on our own way – some paired off and others walked in smaller clusters, each focused on reaching camp for our final night on the mountain.

It was tough.

From Base Camp to Mweka Camp took us about eight hours. We trickled in – some just before sunset, others well after dark. We had summited, yes – but we were completely, utterly spent. All we wanted was our usual bowl of hot water – *kan jy dit glo* (can you believe it) – and food. Our much-loved soup before crawling into our tents.

There were a lot of brave faces hiding how we really felt. No Festo briefing. No chat. Just bowl baths and long silences.

But, Festo had one more surprise up his sleeve.

With dinner, he presented Deb with a proper birthday cake. It wasn't practical to haul it to higher camps, but he'd planned ahead. A simple gesture. A perfect dessert. And a reminder of who we were again – people, friends, not just climbers running on empty.

That night, something swung around. For once, the group turned the tables on Festo.

He was known for saying things like, "I am begging you… I beg you – for a 5am start, a 4:30am wake-up?"

But this time, it was our team doing the begging. The summit was behind us. The mountain had wrung every bit of energy out of us. What we needed now was simple – a long sleep.

We negotiated a 7:30am wake-up for Day 8 on the mountain.

And it felt like a *win*.

After days of '*pole pole*,' early starts and pushing through discomfort, sleeping in was our first small luxury on the way back to normal life. Not quite Springlands Hotel yet, but closer.

We knew we'd made it. The climb was behind us. The summit, the descent, the altitude, the layers, the tears, the laughs, and the sweat. All of it.

Now, it was time to reflect. To recover. **And soon, to celebrate – even if not the way we'd expected.**

Team Reflections – The Descent

Belinda

Of course, the trek was not without its challenges, maneuvering steep descents and managing the strain on my knees and toes was no small feat. Still, I am profoundly grateful for the opportunity to climb Kilimanjaro alongside the rest of the team and our support crew from Zara. Reflecting on my past adventures, nothing quite compares to the experience of Kili. Drawing from my previous altitude hikes, I understood the essentials for success: fueling my body, staying hydrated, prioritizing rest and maintaining a healthy mindset.

Peter

Descent from the summit back to base camp was far more of a challenge than I had ever anticipated. Although I felt physically fine and had no obvious signs of altitude illness or nausea, my balance on the now rapidly melting ice was abominable. Although, not a drinker, anyone witnessing my attempt at descent that morning could easily be forgiven for suspecting I had just drained my third bottle of Jack Daniels in ten minutes. My inability to balance on the way from the summit to base camp was something I had not foreseen and am still to this day at a loss to explain.

Jenny

After slipping and sliding, for 4 hours, down the mountain back to base camp, to pack up the tents, we thought it would be a relatively easy day, but it turned out to be brutal. It was 7 more hours of stepping down huge stairs of what could almost be described as waterfall track.

Libby

Snow and ice seemed rare when researching what to expect but were very real for our summit day. After 12 hours hiking on only 90 minutes of sleep, the descent was the ultimate test of my physical limits. I would not have made it without my amazing Maasai companion. My water bottle and backpack were taken from me to help, but they also made it harder for me to stay hydrated.

Parched, after a short stop at Base Camp, we had to keep going. The uneven, rocky and steep steps were the final, unrelenting exclamation point when we made it to our final camp an hour after dark, almost 21 hours after we started our journey to the summit.

Deb

We had been advised to train for it – but nothing could prepare me for this brutal section. Already exhausted beyond understanding, I had to navigate slick ice, melting snow slush, uneven ground, and sucking mud patches. Every step requires focus. No respite.

Eventually, I reached Mweka Camp, with only 2 hours to eat, pack, adjust gear and head off again – another 7km ahead. The first 4km was not too harsh, thanks to rain settling the dusty lava field. Another nosebleed. Then dusk fell and we began the most insidious track I have ever traversed: concrete steps with fist-sized rocks jutting out.

Ankle-snapping terrain. Hips, knees, ankles screaming. Two headlamps between five of us. Every step assessed in the dark.

We reached camp an hour after nightfall – ending a 26-hour day with only 1.5 hours of interrupted sleep. Too exhausted to fully appreciate the birthday cake and bottle of wine offered on this remote and challenging mountain. Surreal.

"You never really leave the mountain. It stays with you – in your breath, your pace, your story."

– Anonymous

CHAPTER 10

THE ECHO AFTER THE CLIMB: THE QUIET DESCENT

The morning after the summit, the mountain had one surprise for us.

In the days leading up to it, we'd learned that singing by the porters was no longer allowed on the mountain. It surprised us. Most of us had seen those cheerful clips on YouTube – porters dancing in camp, welcoming climbers with songs full of rhythm and heart. It was one of the things we thought we'd experience. Even quietly hoped for. Something uniquely Kilimanjaro.

Turns out, the rule was new. The explanation given was that singing disturbed other climbers trying to rest or sleep at altitude. Fair enough – but it still felt like something had been taken away. That made Deb's special 'Happy Birthday' serenade a couple of days earlier even more meaningful. It was allowed because we weren't in a designated camp when we stopped for morning tea. The moment wasn't just special for Deb – we all soaked it up. The rareness of it somehow made it better.

What we didn't know, what Festo had secretly kept up his sleeve, was that singing was allowed in the camps after summiting. And he'd saved it for just the right moment.

After our summit night and that brutal descent, we slept in until 7:30am – a proper lie-in on the mountain. Some of us even bragged it was our best night's sleep. That 3cm-thick roll-out mattress suddenly didn't feel so thin. I reckon I clocked ten straight hours. No pit stops. Just deep, uninterrupted sleep at 3,000 metres. That alone felt worth celebrating.

We moved differently that morning, as we rolled up sleeping bags and packed gear for the last time before breakfast. The climb was behind us. It was no longer about conquering. We were still tired, but somehow lighter. Now it was about recovery; hot showers, a cold beer, maybe a massage.

Then, just as we were lacing boots and stuffing daypacks, ready to begin the final descent, Festo called everyone together.

The ten of us gathered. The porters were already standing in a loose semicircle, waiting. And then... they started singing.

An African surprise celebration.

Their voices filled the crisp morning air – clapping, rhythm, dancing, and joy pouring out of tired bodies. It caught us off guard in the best possible way. It felt like a celebration not just of the summit, but of everything that had come before. Honest, pure and full of soul.

That moment is why we have over 80 videos between us, more than a third capturing the singing. It moved us, deeply. We joined in, dancing and singing without a care in the world. One of those rare moments where joy just takes over... and you go with it. Exhausted, emotional, sunburned, aching... but smiling, laughing, clapping along.

The singing naturally set the stage for speeches. We all wanted to say something. To thank Festo and his team. For leading us with strength, with heart. There were tears. There were words that mattered. Sincere gratitude poured out from every one of us.

Then, with our hearts full of the surprise celebration, we slung on our packs and began the final walk off the mountain. A memory we will carry for life.

Mweka Camp to National Park Gate

The hike to the National Park Gate wasn't exactly short. It took us three and a half hours to descend 800 metres over 10 kilometres: a gradual drop of about 80 metres per kilometre. That steady slope helped loosen us up after what we'd put our bodies through the day before.

For the first time, we saw the mountain stretcher – a single-wheel contraption flanked by six porters, racing down the trail with a climber who needed medical attention. It was confronting. Every bump and jolt brought cries of pain from the troubled climber. We hadn't seen it on the way up, probably because the descent followed a different path. Smart, really. The route up already had the unavoidable daily helicopter noise that reminded us of what could go wrong. This was something else.

Our group had done remarkably well. Nothing too serious affected anyone. Sure, there were a few bouts of diarrhoea, some nausea, one person vomiting and one needing assistance with the descent due to balance issues. But overall? We managed. I credit Festo's leadership, the eight days on the mountain, months of diligent training, Diamox, painkillers, good food, and great group dynamics. It all came together. It worked.

Reaching the gate and spotting the bus felt glorious. Sitting down to lunch was even better. We took another group photo in front of the

"Congratulations" sign. Another reminder of what we'd just achieved. We'd finished the eight-day Lemosho Route. All ten of us.

Back on the Bus

Back on the bus, the ride to the hotel felt shorter. Spirits were high. We started sharing photos and videos, reliving the moments. At the same time, everyone was longing for the same thing – a hot shower. Some of us even rang ahead to make sure the hot water was turned on in our rooms. A few booked much-needed massages for that afternoon.

About 15 minutes from the hotel, Festo started singing again; this time joined by Geoffrey, Monday and a few others. But this round was different. They sang our names, one by one, giving each of us a gift of handmade beads to wear around our necks. It was personal. Playful. Moving. Even the schoolchildren we drove past walking home smiled – probably familiar with seeing sunburnt foreigners singing after summiting Kilimanjaro.

More joy. And for me, a heart full of gratitude, that went beyond words.

Back at the Hotel

Back at the Springlands Hotel, after a much-needed hot shower and after returning our hired gear, we gradually gathered in the courtyard late that afternoon for a drink. Eventually, all ten of us were there – together one last time with Festo and his immediate team.

He stepped forward to present our certificates – official documents from Zara Tours and Kilimanjaro National Park. One for each of us. Ten names. Ten rectangles of thin paper that somehow carried the weight of what we'd climbed and who we'd become in the process.

It felt strange. Same hotel. Same staff. But we were different. Cleaner. Hungrier. Grateful in a way we hadn't been ten days earlier. Festo called out our names one by one, handing over the certificates with genuine pride. Even the team leaders seemed chuffed – they'd helped ten climbers reach the top and it showed.

No long speeches. Just a shared understanding of what it meant.

The mosquitoes were back now; a reminder that we'd returned to lower altitude.

We paused for more photos – proof, perhaps. But also, to congratulate one another again. That night, over our final dinner together, the pressure was gone. The mountain was behind us. What remained was the group – a team who had said yes to the same challenge and stuck with it, step by step.

The conversation turned naturally to highlights. What stood out. What mattered. And more than half the group said the same thing: the best part wasn't the summit, it was the journey. The whole eight months: The training, the chats, the commitment, the shared momentum. There was a quietness to it all. Not sadness. Just a deep sense of something completed.

The Other Victory – Group Dynamics

As I sat back at dinner that night, I realised something else worth mentioning. Ten people. Eight days. No showers. Thin air. Sleep deprivation. Sore knees, sore toes, and sore everything. Maybe even a few *'lost personalities'* along the way – to borrow Belinda's now famous phrase. And yet, nothing ugly had spilled out. No blow-ups. No sulks. No fractures in the group. That in itself felt like a victory.

Sure, there were moments when each of us had to take a deep breath and adjust to the different ways people approached things. That's part of travelling in any group. But no one wanted to be the difficult person. I once heard someone say, *"If you don't know who that person is… it might be you."* A sobering thought.

But the real beauty was this: we looked out for each other, regardless of our differences. We listened, we laughed, we gave each other space when it was needed. That unspoken commitment to the group – that's what held it together. That's what made it work.

For me, having my own tent was a godsend, an idea that was flagged by a few in the group during our training months. It gave me a place to crawl into at night, journal and reset. I did think to myself that the couples in their two persons tent's might have appreciated two single tents the odd night as well. Space is underrated at altitude.

Looking around that table, I realised we had done something remarkable. We'd not only climbed Africa's highest mountain – we had carried ten very different personalities through a pressure cooker of fatigue and discomfort without losing respect or humour. That, as much as the summit, was worth celebrating.

The Next Morning – Goodbyes & Dr Haggai

The next morning, we began to part ways. Some flew directly home. Others headed to Zanzibar for a few days; a popular place for Kilimanjaro climbers to decompress. A few set off on planned safaris. The goodbyes unfolded over the next 24 hours.

First to go were Dan, and then Andy and Dave – out by 9am, off on a Qatar flight straight back to Brisbane. No fuss. Classic. Quick hugs, shoulder claps, maybe a cheeky grin from Dave and they were gone, like the efficient unit they'd been all climb long.

Next were Deb, Belinda and Libby. Off to Zanzibar for proper wind-down time; swims, massages, market stalls, and slow mornings.

They'd earned it. It made sense they'd decompress together. They'd been close on the mountain too. This gave them space to laugh, relive stories and let the climb settle gently.

That left a few of us for one final lunch together – Peter, Jenny, John and me.

Before lunch I'd received a call from Mama Zara. She was in Sweden, waiting on an operation of her own, yet still reached out. Calm as ever, she asked about the summit, the team and my return to Moshi. Then she told me about a small preschool she'd founded for three-to-five-year-olds – part of her vision to give children a better start before primary school.

I was invited to visit and I'm so glad I said yes.

I managed to fit in the visit just before lunch. February 2nd – now etched in my memory as "A Special Day." Her school principal took me into town to see the school for myself: four classrooms, two already full of about fifty children and two still under construction. It was a Saturday, so no students were there, but the place was still full of colour, care and purpose. A real, tangible legacy – being built in the shadow of the mountain. Her vision to keep children off the street left a mark on me.

Then – just as lunch was being served – in walked Dr Haggai. A surprise guest.

And then – in walked Dr Haggai. A surprise guest.

I hadn't seen him since the medical emergency over a year earlier. It was one of those full-circle moments you don't see coming. He looked proud, relaxed, genuinely happy to see me, looking a whole lot stronger than when he first met me, catheter and all.

After the five of us had lunch, we chatted. I brought him up to date on everything: the successful surgery, the recovery, the summit. He seemed genuinely pleased, even quietly proud. Rightly so. He encouraged me to write a book about it all. We took a photo and shared a hug that said more than words. It was one of those moments that solidified everything that had just happened – a quiet reminder of how far I'd come.

That evening, John and I packed our things for our own Qatar flight the next day. More goodbyes. More hugs. We said farewell to Peter and Jenny, who were just beginning their safari adventure. They'd timed it well – mountain first, then rest and wonder. After our flight to Doha, I said goodbye to John, who had a connecting flight back home to Brisbane – while I stayed behind for stopover.

It was strange being alone again. The WhatsApp group was still pinging, of course – beach updates from Zanzibar, safari photos, delayed flights, blurry selfies in Doha. But the noise around me had changed. No more group laughter. No more tent zips at 3am. No more shared mission.

I went from walking in step with others to walking through an airport alone. Sore legs and a head full of slow-burning realisations.

The Post-Event Blues

A couple of weeks after getting home, I gave Moo a call to see if she could make it to the reunion we had planned for the 5th of April 2025. We hadn't spoken since before the climb. She let me know she was caring for her nieces and couldn't make it, then she casually asked, "So… how's the post-event blues going?"

I paused. The question hit me harder than I expected. I hadn't named it yet, but the moment she said it, something clicked. I went, *Ahh… that's exactly what I've been feeling.* It made sense coming from Moo. With all her travel and adventure, she knew the highs and lows that follow big journeys. Moo helped me realise there was something else going on – something more than just jet lag.

It wasn't depression. It felt more like coming down from a high. A kind of withdrawal. Something missing. Even though I'd physically landed back in Australia, my mind was elsewhere, somewhere else… still back in Africa.

I'd been home for weeks, but I still hadn't really landed. Life had technically resumed – work, appointments, emails, bills – but I wasn't fully in it. I was struggling to find my rhythm again. A big part of me didn't want to slot back in. I was craving the next thing. If I'm honest, I missed the high; the simplicity, the clarity, the buzz of doing something big with others. It's a drug. And I was coming down.

So, I did a bit of research and discovered this feeling has a name. Psychologists call it *post-event letdown* or *post-adventure blues;* a common emotional dip after intense, meaningful experiences. It shows up in elite athletes after the Olympics, performers after big tours, newlyweds after the wedding… and yes, climbers after conquering the summit.

Turns out, it can last for days, or even weeks. It's your body and mind trying to recalibrate after running on adrenaline, purpose and connection.

For me, it was weeks. I'd handled the jet lag fine. But I hadn't understood what I was feeling until Moo's question. Thanks, Moo.

During the climb, everything had been stripped back. One job. One team. One mountain. Then you come home and suddenly, you have to resume attending to the essential, mundane stuff of real life. The contrast is jarring.

A 2019 study in the *Journal of Applied Sport Psychology* looked at elite athletes after major competition. It found a consistent emotional crash post-event. Even when the event was a success – or *especially* when it was – athletes reported feeling flat, aimless, emotionally unanchored. One Aristotle quote stood out to me: "The intensity of the lead-up creates a vacuum in the come down."

That's exactly it.

You live with that build-up for months – training, planning, visualising – and then, in a moment, it's over. The WhatsApp group goes quiet. The adrenaline fades. The mountain's behind you. And you're left wondering… *now what?*

The good news? It passes. Slowly, your normal life takes root again. You begin to absorb what you did. The story becomes part of you. But in those in-between weeks, the transition is real. And I wasn't ready for it. I wasn't stuck. I was just adjusting.

And then came the reunion. Perfect timing, really. It gave shape to the strange in between space – a chance to reconnect, reflect and remember.

The Reunion & Reflections

On the 5th of April 2025, we had our reunion. Partners were invited. We'd chosen the date so Libby could be there. She was going to be in Brisbane that weekend and it just made sense to plan around it. One more WhatsApp interaction, like old times.

It had been ten weeks since our arrival in Moshi to summit Kilimanjaro. In some ways, it felt like a lifetime ago, even though it had only been a little over two months.

The vibe was relaxed. Laughter came easy. Dave turned up with a bunch of white roses, one for each person, clearly trying to redeem himself after the April Fools' prank, he'd pulled just days earlier. He'd posted a message in the group chat claiming he'd seriously injured himself at work; something about a fall, scans and painkillers. Everyone jumped in with sympathy, offering help. And then… "April Fool!" Let's just say it didn't land quite as gently as he'd hoped.

The roses were his peace offering, a way of saying sorry without saying sorry. Classic Dave. At least, he wasn't sneaking rocks into people's daypacks.

Across the centre of the long table, we'd laid out about 100 printed photos from our eight-month journey; training hikes, mountain moments, funny mishaps, everything in between. A great way to remind ourselves and one another, of the whole story. The photos were passed around like treasure. We couldn't stop smiling. The memories felt close again.

There was something familiar about the night. It reminded me of a matric (short for matriculation, the final year of high school in South Africa) school reunion. That unspoken connection you have with people you've been through something big with, even if life has since pulled you in different directions. It wasn't about planning the next thing. It was about remembering something we did together – something that still mattered.

It was like the embers of a fire that once blazed; soft, glowing, still giving off warmth.

Unlike the group I'm part of – the Aging Elite Athletes – where we pick a new challenge each year to train for, commit to and tick off together. Kilimanjaro was different. This challenge didn't come from a group searching for what's next. It *created* a group – a group of people who felt the same tug at the same time and said yes. That's what made it unique.

We caught up on things we hadn't had the chance to share; stories from the mountain, the trip home, recovery. Each of us remembered something different, but all of it pointed to the same truth – the mountain had left a mark.

A few were already researching the next challenge. Not because they were chasing the same high, but because they'd tapped into something – the joy of shared effort, of pushing past limits, of doing something that mattered with people who mattered.

The WhatsApp group was still alive. Photos from the reunion went up that night. There were more jokes about Dave's roses. But mostly, there was gratitude; not just for the summit, but for the amazing and beautiful group of people who said yes to the same mountain at the same time.

What's Next

No one said it out loud at the reunion, but the question was there, floating just beneath the smiles, the hugs, the stories: **So... what's next?**

Adventure was already in our veins. Many of us hadn't just climbed a mountain – we'd climbed out of something. A rut. A restless season of life that needed shaking up. Something inside had stirred, and it wasn't going back to sleep. This wasn't just a box-tick adventure. It was, for most of us, an answer to an earlier question. And that's why the come down can feel so confronting. You reach the top, you descend... and then what?

The WhatsApp group had already lit up with new ideas: Everest Base Camp, Kokoda, the Larapinta Trail, even a slow meander across the South Island of New Zealand. The momentum was still alive. So was the purpose. The reason to train again. To pack a bag again.

I encourage you – the reader – to find your next one. These moments help you rediscover life balance, forge friendships and gather experiences that make you reflect on what really matters. And when you do – ask yourself: *who with?* Because that's what creates the lifetime memories.

"If you want to go fast, go alone. If you want to go far, go together."
– African Proverb

In the closing chapter, I'll share how it changed me – what I learned in the space between losing something and finding something else entirely.

I am deeply grateful – because **adventure really does have a way of reminding you who you are and what truly matters in life.**

Team Reflections – The Celebration

Libby

One of the highlights was celebrating with our large support crew on our last morning. Many had worked behind the scenes and were not known to us until now. The singing and dancing were infectious.

Dave

Kilimanjaro was a long-held dream of mine. Andy and I had tried to organize a climb over a decade ago, but it never happened. I am grateful to Michael for inviting me to join the team and it was fantastic to have Andy come too. Before the trip Andy told me, *"I really wanna have fun on this journey."* So, I made it my mission to help him – with a few pranks that may have stretched the friendship! Thankfully, he seems to have forgiven me.

Despite the playful teasing, our team bonded quickly. Our guides were exceptional – especially Festo, who nicknamed me *Babu* (Grandpa in Swahili). He was encouraging, protective and humorous throughout.

The chill was immense, but not even freezing toes, thin air, or sleep deprivation could stop our determined upward climb. Reaching the summit was truly unforgettable and I am grateful for the friendships and memories forged on this incredible journey.

Dan

Back in 2018, on my way to a safari in Tanzania, we flew past the majestic Kilimanjaro, its summit poking just above the clouds – a sight that left me in awe. At that moment, I never imagined I would one day stand atop that incredible mountain.

However, with Belinda's encouragement, the dream of returning to Tanzania and tackling Kilimanjaro began to feel like a real possibility.

This achievement would not have been possible without the unwavering support of our amazing guides, for which I am profoundly grateful. Their expertise was invaluable, and I could not have asked for better companions on this trip. I also must give a special shout-out to the food – nothing quite compares to the comfort of a Snickers bar on summit day – and, of course, sharing this adventure with Belinda made it even more special.

Reaching the summit was a testament to the hard work I put into my training, ensuring I prepared properly for the challenges of the mountain and maintaining a positive mindset throughout the experience.

The most significant takeaway from hiking Kilimanjaro is that with determination and commitment, so much more is achievable.

Deb

After a restorative sleep and satisfying breakfast, we were honored with speeches, songs and dancing. The crew were proud to have assisted all ten of us with reaching Stella Point – and seven Uhuru Summit.

A well-graded trail through the rainforest led to the final stretch along a gravel road – which somehow did the most damage to my feet. All my own fault: I did not tighten my boots after downsizing from three to one pair of socks. Too shattered, too lazy to adjust and adapt.

But blisters heal faster than hearts.

And my once-weary heart is now full, whole and bursting with satisfaction.

John

Climbing Kilimanjaro for me was a life-changing experience and, without exception, the most challenging thing I have ever done, both physically and mentally.

I came late to the training hikes the rest of the group had been doing for some months, only joining them in November. I knew I needed to get much fitter to 'last the distance.' As an athlete, I had excelled in sprints and jumps and some team sports – but definitely not endurance activities.

At 70 years of age, I was also the oldest member of the party by 7 years and 15 or so years older than the youngest. I did not want to be a liability. I was gym fit but not Kilimanjaro fit. With an elevated heart rate, I doubted my ability to summit, so through December I hit the gym daily, working on aerobic fitness. The stepper became my 'frenemy.' By mid-January I felt stronger and that maybe I had a chance!

I wouldn't have succeeded if it hadn't been for my friends, Festo and some of his leaders. On day three, Festo must have realized that I would need extra help. "Papa John, would you mind if I carry your day pack and water?" From then on, either he or one of his leaders did so. I felt humbled, particularly by the profound respect and honour I was shown (probably – due to my age!). I would not have made the last few hundred meters to Stella Point if Festo and one of his leaders hadn't come running down the slope to support me and take an arm on either side. The credit for any success goes to his incredible sensitivity and caring leadership.

My WHY for climbing Kilimanjaro came from my desire to get my life 'unstuck.' Through various circumstances, I had become rather over-whelmed and felt like I had little agency or momentum to bring positive change. Kilimanjaro was a chance to break this pattern and lay hold of life in a fresh way. So, I took a Tanzanian flag with me on the climb with a new 'life statement'!
It is NOT 'it is what it is' – it IS what you MAKE it!
Climbing Kilimanjaro for me was a watershed that has given me the agency and momentum in this new year that I so desperately needed. I am deeply grateful to Festo and my group of mountain friends, who helped to make this possible.

CONCLUSION /
EPILOGUE

REFLECTIONS FROM A DREAM FINALLY REALISED

Thank you for coming this far with me.
Writing this book has been its own adventure –
at times cathartic, often challenging,
but always worthwhile.

Sharing it with you has made it even more meaningful.

As we bring things to a close,
I'd like to step back and share what I believe
was really at work through it all –
and why the story isn't finished yet.

CHAPTER 11

✥

A LIFE FOREVER CHANGED

Beyond Serendipity: The God-Incidents in My Story

He has shown you, O mortal, what is good.
And what does the Lord require of you?
To act justly and to love mercy and to walk humbly with your God.
– Micah 6:8 (NIV)

O ver the years, I've had a few wake-up calls in life, but none louder than the one that came out of my Serengeti experience in Tanzania, in the middle of Africa.

One I'm incredibly grateful for!

Like my 30th birthday wake-up call, it triggered a shift in how I approach life. But this one was different. The forty-hour ordeal in December 2023 – my first trip to climb Kilimanjaro – came with a medical emergency, the detour, the waiting and everything that unfolded. It wasn't just about a change in my adventure plans.

It was about life itself.

It woke me up to the deeper things of life – the things that matter most. To faith. To family. To friendships. To my mortality – the reality that our tomorrows are not promised. When life is going well, it's easy to forget those earlier days when I walked closely with God, when His goodness felt so tangible and constant. In the years leading up to this trip, I had drifted more than I realised. Not deliberately, but slowly – letting busyness, disappointments and even successes crowd out my daily conversations with Him in prayer.

Earlier that same year, I remember an evening with the card buddies. No card night is ever the same – I honestly think we've covered just about every topic under the sun over the years. But this night was different. The game slowed, the cards rested on the table and the conversation turned to past God-incidents in our lives as Christians. One by one, we shared stories we could recall. It left us all deeply inspired.

Driving home after another midnight finish, I couldn't shake the thought: I want to see more of that. More of God's handiwork, like the stories we'd just shared, like the miracles I'd witnessed as a young man in Africa. That night stirred something in me – a yearning that hasn't gone away. I may be over sixty now, but I still feel young. Younger than my years. Why shouldn't I keep looking for more?

Little did I know that less than a year later I'd have another story to add – one I'll never forget. There was a moment when I knew, instantly, that God was with me. Not later in hindsight, but right there in real time. The hairs on the back of my neck stood up.

You know the one I'm referring to – my unexpected lunch with Mario, the urologist from Germany. While I sat there with a catheter in and the urine bag strapped to my thigh. Yes, wow. He gave me the knowledge I needed about the exact procedure I required back in Australia. That moment carried me through the uncertainty that followed.

I was experiencing a series of God-incidents – significant events that are hard to explain as mere coincidences.

As a believer for almost forty-five years – I became a Christian in my final year of high school on the 1st of November 1980 – I don't see that lunch with Mario as serendipity, luck, or coincidence. It was a divine appointment, orchestrated by a loving God. I knew instantly God was with me, looking after me – an incredibly humbling, comforting and moving experience.

Even the long flight home – five flights over five days – became a gift. With the emergency behind me, I could finally pause, reflect and take note of His handiwork. On the flight from Dar es Salaam to Muscat, I had a quiet moment holding back tears, realising just how much He was carrying me through it all. Those quiet days of travel gave me the unexpected space to absorb what had just happened.

Looking back now, I can't explain away more than a dozen separate events as coincidence. I'm sure there are even more I haven't seen – things He put in place long before I even cried out for help that morning, sitting in the front of that Toyota Cruiser in the Serengeti, wondering how on earth I was going to survive a whole day's drive to get the medical help I needed.

My faith clearly sees these for what they are: God-incidents – not coincidences, not serendipity, not luck…

And as I have carefully shared throughout this book, I can now look back and trace His fingerprints across so many things:

- **Mama Zara's upgrade** – the only reason I met the doctor onsite in the middle of the Serengeti.
- **The airport stop** – the first stop was the one place I needed to be to fly out, rather than drive further, another who knows how many hours.

- **Dr Haggai's care** – personally picking me up from the Springlands Hotel, taking me to the nurse for a scan and then to his clinic for the catheter.
- **The nurse's availability** – able to see me within an hour of my return to Moshi to confirm the enlarged prostate and fluid build-up.
- **The visiting surgeon** – in town at the right moment, with the exact silicon catheter I needed in his doctor's bag.
- **Mama Zara's kindness** – offering me the chance to return later to still climb Kilimanjaro, after my flights had been brought forward, which kept my focus on coming back.
- **Lunch with Mario** – a free consultation at Springlands Hotel, where he explained the robotic prostatectomy. I flew home with knowledge that felt like a divine appointment.
- **Perfect flight timing** – leaving the afternoon I said goodbye to Michelle and Anton and arriving on a Sunday – just in time for further tests with my urologist.
- **The delay in reaching my urologist** – which led me to research and discover Dr Kua, who ultimately performed the robotic prostatectomy.
- **A friend's phone call** – opening the door for me to see Dr Kua two days later for an urgent appointment.
- **The open theatre** – Dr Kua fitting in extra operations on Sunday 17 December, just three days after my appointment.
- **My birthday milestone** – the catheter removed so soon on my 61st birthday, less than 20 days after it had first been put in on the other side of the world.

- **Full restoration** – a successful operation, a healthy recovery, no cancer and normal life back – even the simple joy of swatting flies on the wall again.

And that was only the beginning. As I shared my story, other God-incidents became clear:

- **Coffee with Deb** – in February 2024, a simple catch-up that sparked the ripple effect leading to the group of ten who climbed in January 2025.
- **Altitude training in South Africa** – time with brother-in-law Anton and my nephews, a priceless gift.
- **The Mount Fuji plan** – August 2025, another climb, this time with my sister and her son.

Even writing this book has carried its share of God-incidents – nudges of encouragement, unexpected conversations at business breakfasts, an introduction to a publisher through a friend, an invitation to a book launch and random texts from mates when the writing got tough. With dyslexia, I've leaned on voice software, editors, ChatGPT, friends and family. The timing of that encouragement? I believe that was God at work – and I'm grateful.

And it wasn't just in the writing. It's hard to put into words how many people contributed to this journey – people who, in their own way, helped me up the mountain and safely back down again. These challenges bring humility. You realise quickly no one climbs alone. Yes, you train. Yes, you prepare. But the summit is never just your own – it's built on the shoulders of others. Thank you.

You can't walk away from all this unchanged. Yes, I summited Kilimanjaro – but the real story is everything before and after and the adventure of walking with God that continues still. At the very centre of it all, my deepest gratitude is to Him.

Literally overnight, I was back in the Word, opening my much-loved, blue-covered Bible that has travelled with me for decades. I've always remembered to pack it, though the toothbrush had seen more daily use in recent years. Now, more than eighteen months later, I begin each morning with prayer and end evenings in His Word – living my faith actively again.

And that is what's changing me. I've realised the mountain was only ever part of the story. What truly matters is what comes after – where gratitude turns into legacy, where adventure is found in living fully and where the greatest adventure of all is walking daily with Him, following His will.

Thank You, Father God.

Men's Health Matters

"Being vulnerable is not a weakness – it's a strength."
– Dwayne "The Rock" Johnson

There's been a shift – and it's long overdue.

More men are starting to talk. About their health. About getting checked. About the things we used to keep a secret – prostate issues, mental health, heart checks, weight gain, sleep, libido, energy levels – all of it. There's a growing awareness that the old school *"she'll be right"* attitude doesn't hold up, especially after forty.

And that's a good thing.

To be fair, I wasn't ignoring my health. I'd been doing regular check-ups for years. I already knew I had a benign enlarged prostate. I had mates I could talk to – especially in the Elite Athletes – where the conversation might start with training, or recovery, but often landed on deeper stuff. We'd talk about blood pressure, injuries, testosterone, energy levels, whatever was going on. Nothing too dramatic, but enough to keep it honest.

Then there is the Card Buddies. Different setting, different rhythm – but the same foundation – trust, humour, history. Sure, we'd start the night focused on who was winning the next hand of 500, but somewhere between the Amarula and the boerewors, someone would throw in a health update. A procedure. A new supplement. A "Mate, you need to get that checked". Often followed by laughter, but the kind of laughter that says, *we get it.*

So, when things went sideways for me in the Serengeti, it wasn't because I'd let things slide. It was just one of those moments that escalated fast. A known condition, suddenly in the wrong place at the wrong time. No hospital nearby. No urologist. Just a body that stopped cooperating and a trip that had to be cut short.

That's the thing about health… Even when you're on top of it, life can throw a curveball.

What makes a huge difference is whether you've got people around you who'll listen. For me, that was the mates I'd already shared openly with. But here's what I've realised: those regular check-ups? They mattered even more *because* of what happened. Knowing my condition early meant I wasn't walking blind. I had context. And once I got back to Australia, I already had the referrals, the scans, the knowledge base to act quickly.

And the openness with mates? That helped more than I realised.

When you've already had the chat, it's easier to keep talking. I had people I could debrief with. Not just about the mountain, but about my body, the frustration, the catheter, the recovery. It wasn't awkward. It was just life.

Too many men wait until something breaks. We push through. Delay appointments. Hope it'll go away. But if I've learned anything, it's this: being proactive isn't weakness – it's wisdom. It gives you time. Options. Perspective.

Since the surgery, I've spoken more openly than ever. I don't make a big deal out of it – but I also don't hide it. And I've lost count of how many men have quietly pulled me aside to say, "I've got something similar going on", or "I really should get checked".

And let's be honest – this isn't just about *you*. It's about the people who love you. The people who want more birthdays, more holidays, more laughs, more years *with* you. When we take our health seriously, we're not being selfish – we're being responsible. It's one of the most practical ways to show up for the people who matter.

If you're not sure where to start. Back in Chapter 6, I included a quick sidebar with the key check-ups men should be doing by decade – from your 30s through to your 70s. Don't treat it like a chore. Think of it as tuning the engine before the next big climb.

So, if you're reading this and you've been meaning to book that appointment, just do it. Talk to your GP. Mention the thing that's been bugging you. It doesn't have to be a crisis to be worth your attention.

That's the ripple effect. You go first and it gives someone else permission to do the same.

Because this is what health looks like now – shared, proactive and unashamed.

'n Regte man kyk na homself (a real man looks after himself).

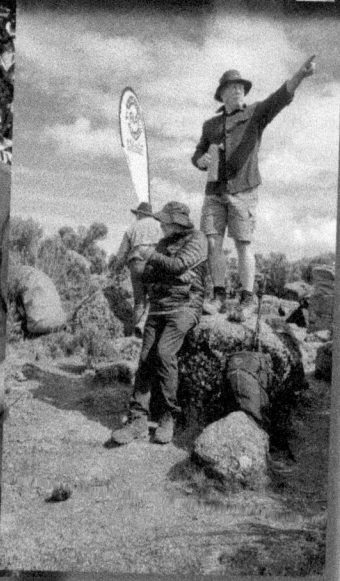

The Adventure Spirit Lives On

"The proper function of man is to live, not to exist. I shall not waste my days in trying to prolong them. I shall use my time."
— Jack London

I first heard that quote, not in a book or on a hiking trail, but in a James Bond film – *No Time to Die* (2021). It came right at the end, after Bond had died, as the team raised a glass of whiskey in his honour. It wasn't overdone – just a sincere moment, a toast and that line.

And it stuck.

It stirred something in me. A reminder that it's possible to stay alive without really living… and that is one of the greatest dangers to silently drifting into existing. It made me sit back and ask myself: *Am I really using my time? Or just filling it?*

Though I only discovered the quote years later, it captured exactly what I'd felt after my 30th birthday. I didn't want life to be defined by routine or autopilot. I wanted memories that would mean something – places, people, laughter, effort. Not just another year ticked off, but years marked by momentum.

And retrospectively now, I'm grateful for that decision.

From hikes through the Drakensberg, to off-road trips with the Elite Athletes. From trail runs and mountain climbs, to card weekends filled with banter and boerewors. From Oman's highest peak to Whitehaven's white sands, the list keeps growing. Not just places visited, but moments lived.

And what I've discovered along the way is this: adventure isn't just about where you go – it's about the change that happens inside you when you say yes. It's the change from *"I wonder if I can…"* to *"I just did!"*

That transformation matters. It rewires something.

You realise you're more capable than you thought. That you're allowed to be bold. That your body can surprise you. That your mind doesn't need permission to try. And that choosing discomfort now and then reminds you that you're still alive.

Of course, there's another side to it too. After a big event – whether it's a mountain, a marathon, or a moment you've built toward for months or even years – there's a drop. Post-event blues are real. You've stretched so far, lived so fully, been part of something so purposeful… and then, almost overnight, it's quiet again. Ordinary life feels a little muted.

I've felt that many times. After Kilimanjaro. After the group disbanded. Even while writing this book. It's not depression – it's just contrast. A natural comedown from the high of shared purpose, momentum and the clarity that comes when your goal is in front of you and everyone's rowing in the same direction.

The adventurous spirit doesn't disappear – it just asks, what's next? For me, that often means putting something small but real in the diary. A climb, a hike, a trip with the Elite Athletes. Or a chance to do something new with family, immediate and extended. These don't have to be epic. What matters is that they're shared. Because the real spirit of adventure isn't just the summit; it's the laughter, the bonds, the memories that carry on long after.

That's why I keep something in the diary – something real. It doesn't have to be huge. Just something that stirs the soul. A challenge. A stretch. A *'what if?'* that makes your stomach flutter a bit. *Jy leef net een keer* (you only live once).

That's how the spirit lives on.

Jack London was right. We're not here just to exist. We're here to live. To use our time well.

Climbing mountains might not be everybody's thing – and that's okay. Adventure takes many shapes. What matters is that you don't settle for just existing, but find the kind of living that makes your heartbeat faster, your soul feel alive and, with God's help, turns even the ordinary into a great adventure.

My brother-in-law's post – it's a good example of how the "Adventure Spirit" lives on...

👉 **Reflections 2025 – Kilimanjaro**

What stood out to me was how inspiring it is to see others face their obstacles and push through. To make matters worse, there was an incredible blizzard in the last hour, with almost no visibility even after sunrise. The chill factor dropped the temperature to around -15°C, conditions the guides said were highly unusual for that time of year.

The descent was another adventure altogether. It felt more like skiing each of us arm-hooked to a guide, taking long, fast strides and digging our heels in to stop slipping at every step. It was like fleeing a "survival ordeal" as quickly as possible. 😵 😄

This was a truly fantastic experience. Special thanks to you and Michelle for making it possible for me. **I had been considering tackling the Andes summit one day (about 1,000m higher),** but I think other bucket list items will come first.

Author My brother-in-law, Anton

Sent from my iPhone

ACKNOWLEDGEMENTS

While I'm thankful for the times we live in – where tools like **voice recognition software** and **ChatGPT** have made a huge difference in bringing this book to completion – I'm more thankful for the many real people who have made it possible.

To anyone who took the time to listen to my story along the way and said, "You need to write a book" – thank you. Your words mattered more than you know. In moments of difficulty, that encouragement kept me going.

To those involved in helping write the book – thank you. To **Ark House Publishing** for believing in this story and bringing it to life. To **Stuart**, from **Ultimate 48 Hour Author**, for mentoring me through the structure and process. To those who **read early drafts**, offered thoughtful feedback, encouraged me to keep writing and believed this story mattered – I'm deeply grateful.

To the **Elite Athletes** and the **Card Buddies** – thanks for years of friendship, challenges, deep laughs and always keeping things real.

To the nine fellow climbers who stood with me on **Kilimanjaro** – **Deb, Belinda, Dan, Libby, Dave, Andy, Peter, Jenny and John** – thank you for sharing the journey, the laughter and the summit. We became a team in the truest sense.

To the medical professionals in **Brisbane – Dr Boon Kua**, thank you for fitting me in before Christmas for the successful operation I needed, for the care shown during my recovery and even calling after your holiday had started. Thank you also to the **staff, nurses and volunteers at Greenslopes and Wesley hospitals** for your professional care – it was world-class and has been mentioned over dinner with friends more than once.

To those in **Tanzania** who played a role in this journey – thank you. **Mama Zara (and the Zara Tours family)**, your compassion, hospitality and belief in the dream of a second chance that changed my story. From the very first upgrade to your personal encouragement, your kindness left a lasting mark. **Dr Haggai**, your swift care and personal involvement went far beyond medicine – lifesaving and unforgettable. **Dr Godwin** and **Dr Alfred**, thank you for your part at crucial moments too. **Dr Mario Hanke**, our unplanned lunch together at Springlands Hotel was one of those remarkable moments of timing – your clarity and guidance gave me confidence that recovery and another climb were possible. **Erasto**, thank you for quietly making things happen in the background – your coordination made both attempts possible. And to **Festo**, our head guide and the entire **Zara team** – porters, cooks and crew – you carried not just our bags, but the heart of our journey. The summit wouldn't have been possible without you.

To my wider family – **Michelle and Anton, Joubert, Riaan, Ruben and Duncan** – thank you for the ways you walked this journey with me. Michelle, your courage and companionship from the very beginning helped ignite this dream. **Anton du Plooy**, your willingness to train, climb and dream thousands of miles away from me – from the first Kilimanjaro attempt to the Drakensberg with your sons and our nephew Ruben – left a deep mark. And to **Joubert, Riaan, Ruben and**

Duncan – sharing those mountains with you made unforgettable memories. To my **mother, siblings, brothers and sisters in-law, nephews and nieces** – thank you for your interest, support and encouragement from all corners of the world.

To my wife and children – **Vicki, Michelle and Rodrigo, Timothy and Holly** – your love, encouragement and belief in me were felt every step of the way. **Vicki**, thank you for standing beside me through the setbacks and the detour and for backing me to try again. **Michelle and Rodrigo, Timothy and Holly** – thank you for walking this journey with me. Your support, messages of encouragement meant more than I can say. I didn't climb alone – I love you all.

Above all, I thank **God** – for life, for salvation, for second chances and for the grace to keep going when things didn't go to plan. **Jesus**, my Lord and Saviour, my anchor and my hope. And **Holy Spirit**, who whispered truth and gave me peace – even in the darkest moments – I am forever grateful.

This journey has reminded me again and again: I do not walk alone. With a full heart, thank you all.

– **Michael Delport**
Email: michael@serengetiserendepity.com
www.serengetiserendipity.com

www.ingramcontent.com/pod-product-compliance
Lightning Source LLC
Chambersburg PA
CBHW030923090426
42737CB00007B/295